Fundamentals for the Aspiring Musician

Fundamentals for the Aspiring Musician is a complete, integrated learning resource covering the essential foundations of music. Rather than using separate recording sets or software programs, it integrates a textbook with an interactive, multimedia electronic version on CD-ROM, which enables students and instructors to listen to musical examples and review definitions. It is designed to help students master the basic knowledge and skills of music in preparation for more advanced college music theory studies, while gaining familiarity with some of the most prominent and universally renowned composers and works of the common practice period.

Features

- The CD-ROM is compatible with any computer with a web browser and audio playback capabilities.
- The audio files are embedded *within* the electronic version, rather than in a separate collection on a CD or website.
- Students can hear and practice exercises to master basic skills, easily review and reinforce terms, or delve deeper into a topic with a single click of the mouse.
- End of chapter exercises in the textbook progress from simple to complex, allowing both the student and the instructor to assess the level of mastery of each topic.
- Musical examples are taken from the greatest and richest works of the common practice period. Links to composer biographies are included with examples to build a basic familiarity with the master composers and their works.
- A unique multi-frame interface displays the text, audio playback controls, and definitions in a logical, easy to read format.
- Includes a companion website with student and instructor resources, such as interactive music theory and ear trainers, multiple choice quizzes, flashcards, and an Instructor's Manual.

Robert J. Frank teaches music theory and composition at Southern Methodist University. He has frequently presented his music and is a guest lecturer, nationally and internationally, on the topic of integrating technology into the teaching and making of music.

Kenneth Metz teaches music theory at the University of the Incarnate Word in San Antonio, Texas. An award winning composer, his music has been performed across the United States.

www.routledge.com/textbooks/fundamentalsfortheaspiringmusician

Fundamentals for the Aspiring Musician

A Preparatory Course for Music Theory

Robert J. Frank and
Kenneth Metz

Routledge
Taylor & Francis Group

NEW YORK AND LONDON

First published 2011
by Routledge
270 Madison Avenue, New York, NY 10016

Simultaneously published in the UK
by Routledge
2 Park Square, Milton Park, Abingdon, Oxon OX14 4RN

Routledge is an imprint of the Taylor & Francis Group, an informa business

© 2011 Taylor & Francis

Typeset in Minion by
Florence Production Ltd, Stoodleigh, Devon
Printed and bound in the United States of America on acid-free paper by
Sheridan Books, Inc.

Library of Congress Cataloging in Publication Data
Frank, Robert J.
    Fundamentals for the aspiring musician: A Preparatory Course in
    Music Theory
    Robert J. Frank, Kenneth Metz.
        p. cm.
      Includes bibliographical references.
    1. Music theory—Elementary works.   I. Frank, Robert J., 1961–.
    II. Title.
    MT7.M424 2010
    781.2—dc22   2009033860

ISBN13: 978–0–415–80103–4 (hbk)
ISBN13: 978–0–415–80104–1 (pbk)

Contents

Preface   ix
CD-ROM information   xiv
Acknowledgments   xv

1 Introduction and Basics   **1**

1.1 Introduction   1
1.2 Basics of Sound   2
Chapter Summary   5
Chapter 1 Exercises   6

2 Rhythm and Tempo   **9**

2.1 The Pulse and the Beat   9
2.2 Basic Rhythmic Notation   9
2.3 Beaming   10
2.4 Rests   11
2.5 Tied and Dotted Rhythmic Values   12
2.6 Tuplets   13
2.7 Tempo   14
Chapter Summary   15
Chapter 2 Exercises   16

3 Proportional Value, Meter, and Grouping   **18**

3.1 Relative Proportional Values of Notes and Rests   18
3.2 Proportionate Division and Subdivision in Musical Performance   18
3.3 Simple and Compound Groupings and Meter   19
3.4 Simple Meter   21
3.5 Proportion in Simple Meters   21
3.6 Compound Meter   22
3.7 Beaming in Simple and Compound Meters   23
3.8 Tuplets in Compound Meter   24
3.9 Summary of Common Meter Types   25
3.10 Non-metered Music and the Anacrusis   25
3.11 Advanced Topics: Asymmetrical and Mixed Meter   27
Chapter Summary   28
Chapter 3 Exercises   29

4 Aural Application: Rhythmic Reading and Metric Transcription   **32**

4.1 Rhythmic Reading in Simple Meter   32
4.2 Rhythmic Reading in Compound Meter   36
4.3 Reading Tuplets within Simple Groupings   37
4.4 Reading Tuplets within Compound Groupings   38
4.5 Metric Transcription   38
4.6 Metric Transcription between Simple and Compound Meters   39
4.7 Rhythmic Reduction   40
Chapter Summary   42
Chapter 4 Exercises   43

5 Pitch and the Musical Keyboard   **47**

5.1 Pitch Classes and the Musical Keyboard   47
5.2 Specific Pitch and the Modern Keyboard   49
5.3 Musical Notation using Staves and Clefs   50
5.4 Whole and Half Steps on the Musical Staff   53
5.5 Notating Accidentals   54
5.6 Reading Music Pitches   54
Chapter Summary   55
Note Reading Drill   56
Chapter 5 Exercises   57

6 Chromatic, Modal, and Major Scales   **60**

6.1 The Chromatic Scale   60
6.2 Historical Background: The Modes   61
6.3 The Major Scale   62
6.4 Scale Degree Names   64
Chapter Summary   65
Rhythmic Reading Exercises   66
Chapter 6 Exercises   67

7 Tendency Tones and Minor Scales   **69**

7.1 Tendency Tones   69
7.2 The Natural Minor Scale   70
7.3 The Harmonic Minor Scale   71
7.4 The Melodic Minor Scale   71
7.5 Spelling Minor Scales   72
Chapter Summary   74
Rhythmic Reading Exercises   74
Constant Tempo Drill   75
Chapter 7 Exercises   76

8 Key Signatures   **78**

8.1 Key Signatures for Major Keys   78
8.2 Sharp Keys and the Order of Sharps   79
8.3 Flat Key Signatures and the Order of Flats   79
8.4 Minor Key Signatures   80

8.5 Notating Key Signatures   81
8.6 Relationships between Major and Minor Scales   82
8.7 Memorizing Key Signatures   84
Chapter Summary   87
Rhythmic Reading: Triplets   88
Chapter 8 Exercises   89

9   Aural Application: Sight Singing   **93**

9.1 Fixed Do Solfege   94
9.2 Pitch Class Letter Names   95
9.3 "Movable Do" Solfege for Major Keys   95
9.4 Movable Solfege for Minor Scales   95
9.5 Scale Degree Numbers   97
9.6 Application   98
Chapter Summary   99
Chapter 9 Exercises   100

10   Intervals   **103**

10.1 Types of Intervals   103
10.2 General Intervals   103
10.3 Specific Intervals (Diatonic)   105
10.4 Chromatic Alterations of Intervals   107
10.5 Writing and Recognizing Specific Intervals   109
10.6 Melodic Intervals   111
10.7 Simple and Compound Intervals   112
10.8 Inversion of Intervals   113
10.9 Writing Intervals   115
Chapter Summary   117
Aural Drill: Diatonic Intervals   117
Chapter 10 Exercises   119

11   Triads and Seventh Chords   **122**

11.1 Triads   122
11.2 Seventh Chords   124
11.3 Pop/Jazz Chord Symbols   125
11.4 Roman Numerals   126
11.5 Reduction of Chords   127
Chapter Summary   128
Aural Drill: Diatonic Triads   129
Chapter 11 Exercises   130

12   Inversion of Chords and Figured Bass   **133**

12.1 Inversion of Chords   133
12.2 Figured Bass   133
12.3 Roman Numeral Analysis with Inversion Symbols   136
Chapter Summary   138
Aural Drill: Inversion of Major and Minor Triads   139
Chapter 12 Exercises   140

13 Application to Analysis: Chords and Melody in Musical Practice **142**

13.1 Musical Texture and Harmonic Analysis   142
13.2 Melodic Analysis   148
13.3 Further Thoughts on Analysis   150
Chapter Summary   151
Chapter 13 Exercises   152

Appendix 1: Music Notation and Calligraphy   157
Appendix 2: The Overtone Series and Consonance vs. Dissonance   163
Appendix 3: Terms and Definitions   167
Appendix 4: Supplemental Exercises for Sight Singing and Rhythmic Reading   181

Index   187

Preface

Although the study of music fundamentals has remained basically the same over the years almost everything else around it has changed. Today's students are vastly different from those of even a decade or so ago. Changes in music education at the high school level have cut many, if not most, music theory and fundamentals courses. Pressure on students as performance standards are raised to higher and higher levels has led many private lesson instructors to focus more on learning pieces and technique and less on music theory and historical background. As a result, many more students hoping to major in music in college find they have the talent and technique in performance needed for admission, but lack the training in music fundamentals needed to excel in a typical college music theory course. Many outstanding musicians are familiar with the repertoire they have performed but outside of this circle of experience may know other major works in the literature only as ". . . that piece from the light bulb commercial." Today's student is also more at home on a computer than in a library, and in today's media-rich world of the Internet, the use of a static, lifeless, hard-copy text in teaching a living, aural art form such as music may seem archaic at best. Classroom video presentation systems with high quality audio playback have become one of the strongest tools available to help focus attention, lead discussion, and quickly and clearly present new materials.

The study of music fundamentals for a music major or minor is quite different from that of a non-music student seeking only a general education course. Most existing music fundamentals texts were initially written at a time when music fundamentals courses for music students were not common, so the pedagogy, methodology, examples, and techniques are often more general in nature and focused on the use of external crutches and memory aids (like "Every Good Boy Does Fine" to learn staff line note names in treble clef) rather than the formation of a deep, solid foundation for the study of music theory. Although many have added supplemental CDs, computer software, and other external media, we can all agree that learning best takes place when technology is integrated into a single, seamless package without the worries of compatibility or obsolescence.

Fundamentals for the Aspiring Musician is a completely integrated, interactive textbook on CD-ROM with a parallel hard-copy, written for students wishing to study music professionally.

Our goal for this text and method: to use current technology to its fullest to aid students in the preparation for the study of music theory by laying a thorough and solid foundation of basic music fundamentals, and to help the aspiring music student to become familiar with some of the most important and universal works in the common practice repertoire.

What is Different about Our Format and Materials?

Fundamentals for the Aspiring Musician is unique in its format and method of presentation. Rather than using separate, independent recording sets or software programs, our method of teaching music fundamentals integrates a parallel textbook with an interactive, electronic version on CD-ROM, which includes links for students to review definitions and composers, and listen to musical examples within the text. This enables both non-linear learning and integration of multimedia. Evolving from "Theory on the Web"—Robert Frank's MERLOT (Multimedia Educational Resource for Learning and Online Teaching) acclaimed, interactive website—our book is written to provide a thorough foundation in the fundamentals of tonal music. It is based on hypertext (Hypertext Markup Language, or HTML for short). The electronic version is fully compatible with any desktop, laptop, or tablet computer able to display web pages, and initially requires a CD-ROM drive for installation and use directly off the hard drive.

The two components, the CD-ROM and textbook, work intricately and seamlessly together. Students can hear examples as they see them, practice exercises to master basic skills, and easily review and reinforce terms or delve deeper into a topic with a single click of the mouse, whether in the classroom or at home. It is like having a music tutor beside students as they study. The book has an identical layout to the electronic version for easy reference when away from the computer. This also strengthens learning by allowing note taking, highlighting passages of interest, completing written exercises, and serving as a permanent reference for continued musical studies.

We recommend that instructors use the electronic version as the focus for their teaching via in-class audio/visual playback systems. This is one of the unique instructional features of our method that will make classroom instruction dramatically easier and more effective. The audio files are embedded *with* the printed examples, rather than in a separate collection. Musical examples are heard as originally recorded (not just a piano realization), without the need to cue up recordings. By allowing the computer to serve as the "class accompanist," the instructor is free to sing/play/clap along and provide help to the class along with audio playback, without having to play the example on the keyboard.

Tools for Student Understanding

Once materials have been presented, there are several tools for students to practice and reinforce concepts.

- Terms can be accessed easily via pedagogically placed links in the electronic version and the lookup window, without interrupting the flow of their reading with annoying pop-ups or redirected pages, immediately reinforcing the material.
- An end-of-chapter summary (in both the electronic and printed versions) lists key concepts and terms, with links to definitions to reinforce the concepts.
- Included in the printed textbook are exercises at the end of each chapter, progressing in difficulty. These can be handed in to confirm the mastery of the material.
- Appendices with discussion on music notation and calligraphy, the overtone series, terms and definitions, and supplemental exercises for private or in-class sight singing and rhythmic reading enrich student understanding.

A companion website provides additional "hands-on" drills. We encourage students to practice these and master topics before attempting the written self-assessments in the textbook. The drills allow for immediate feedback and correction of mistakes without the need to wait until the next class period. These exercises include:

- **Pitch identification** on the staff and keyboard with numerous drills reinforcing the grand staff, whole verses half steps, scales and their location on the keyboard.
- **Rhythm**, with rhythmic exercises for one or two hands that allow students listen to the correct playback and adjust the tempo, then have their tapping graded).
- **Intervals**, both written and aural identification progressing from whole verses half steps up to the octave, and chords with written and aural identification.

Many of these drills and exercises may be customized by the student (for example, to focus only on diminished chords, or to include all four triad types,) along with the option to email the results directly to the instructor and/or to print them out. Additionally, there are flashcards, quizzes, and supplemental links to additional sites to speed the memorization process for notes, clefs, key signatures, and the other essential components of a fundamentals course.

http://www.routledge.com/textbooks/fundamentalsfortheaspiringmusician

What is Different about Our Pedagogical Approach

We take a "linear pedagogy" approach with all topics throughout this text, where every topic flows smoothly and directly into the next. Every effort has been made to avoid referring to topics prior to their definition and to constantly reinforce important principles. This not only creates a more direct and confident means of introducing new topics, but also builds upon and strengthens each prior skill. For example:

- Our new "Key Signature Tool"—A fresh and simple approach to learning key signatures, it addresses the age-old problem created by the traditional "circle of fifths" tool: students must memorize their scales and understand intervals and the "perfect fifth" before being able to accurately recreate the circle of fifths, but intervals are rarely and not easily covered prior to the study of key signatures, nor are scales mastered by this point in a fundamentals course. This "chicken-and-the-egg" scenario is avoided by a simpler and more direct tool based upon the order of sharps in the key signature (reinforcing this previously covered material).
- Chapter 3: Proportional Value, Meter, and Grouping—After note values have been introduced, but before division and subdivision of the beat in meters can be mastered, a thorough understanding of how note values relate proportionally to both smaller and larger note values is essential and covered thoroughly in this chapter. End-of-chapter written exercises—These progress from simple to complex, allowing both the student and the instructor to assess the level of mastery of each topic. Then, after each major subject area is covered, Chapters Four, Nine, and Thirteen are devoted to applying the practical aural and written concepts to making and analyzing music. This helps the serious music student by not only making the material more relevant, but also by reinforcing these materials at a level that goes beyond abstract drill-and-practice.
- Musical examples from the classical canon—Rather than relying on folk songs or examples more appropriate to a general education course, musical examples in this text are from some of the greatest and richest works of the common practice period. The links to composer biographies in the electronic version build a basic familiarity with the master composers whose works led to the development of modern tonal theory.

To the Teacher

As an aural art form, it is important not only to read about music, but also to *hear*. Ideally, every music student would read their textbook at a piano or other instrument, playing every single example multiple times, and reinforcing terms with which they are not solidly familiar by looking them up in a glossary or dictionary. However, as any honest student or teacher will tell you, this is rarely the case. In fact, in the early stages of study, hearing musical examples is essential *before* students have learned the skills needed to play them. In the past, this has been a major problem in learning music, requiring the constant tutelage of a skilled musician and restricting the review, study, and practice of materials outside of class.

Our use of an interactive, electronic version of the text allows for dynamic discussion and examination, *while hearing* the basic components of the musical language simultaneously. We recommend that students follow this process:

- Read new materials on the CD-ROM *prior to class*, frequently clicking and clarifying the highlighted terms and listening to examples.
- Engage in classroom discussion, when the discussion of the materials can go beyond simply defining terms and concepts.
- Practice the interactive drills, and review until confident with the concepts.
- Complete end-of-chapter exercises in the textbook and submit for grading.

This process allows students to learn and practice outside of class at their own speed and by the method that works best for them without penalty, with only the final result—the demonstrated mastery of the materials in the written assignments—being graded. This system of learning directly addresses many of the goals and outcomes required by many accrediting organizations in higher education.

An instructor's resource is available on the companion website. Instructors will be able to obtain a password to log in and access additional resources, including answer keys for written exercises, quizzes, and sample class plans for quarters and semesters, all designed to make teaching easier, especially for first-time instructors of this course.

Written in today's language and presented in today's medium, it is our hope *Fundamentals for the Aspiring Musician* in a CD-ROM/textbook package will allow for the faster, simpler, and more thorough mastery of the fundamentals of music, and thereby empower students to confidently continue in their study, appreciation, and making of music.

To the Student

If you are reading this, you may already on your way to becoming a professional musician. We are all surrounded by music every day, so many of the topics covered may be aurally familiar to you. Like learning any language, your speaking and listening skills advance much earlier than your reading and writing skills. However, to advance as a musician, as in any profession, you must be more than familiar with your craft. This integrated electronic textbook is designed to provide the solid foundation in the basics of how music is notated and read, plus the terminology and general skills needed to discuss music at a more advanced level with other professional musicians.

This text is designed to be as easy to use as surfing the web or checking your Facebook page (although we don't recommend doing this during your class!). It is extremely important that you learn not only how the elements of music look on the page, but also how they sound and are used in actual musical compositions.

As you read new material in the CD-ROM, you will notice that new terms are highlighted in blue. These terms are links that, when clicked, will display the definition or other additional materials in the definitions window of the browser. Anytime you are not completely sure of a term: click it. Reinforce it. Master it. This way, each new page will feel solid and help you build confidence as you progress in your studies. The musical examples have audio playback. Listen to them many times until you really know the material (think of how many times you have to hear a piece or song on the radio or an MP3 player before you really *know* it). The links and additional materials in the CD-ROM text also allow you to explore familiar topics in greater depth or review new materials at your speed: *you are in control of your learning.*

In the textbook (hard copy), make notes in the margins, since writing something down is one of the greatest tools for remembering it. Take as much time as you need to master a topic before moving on: your computer is infinitely patient. After studying the materials in the text, work the on-line interactive drills to practice and get immediate feedback to your attempts, then when you feel you are ready, attempt the written exercises that your instructor will assign from the workbook.

Finally, use and apply this new knowledge in your daily musical life. In rehearsals and when talking with your friends and fellow musicians, use the terms you study; in practicing your etudes and pieces on your applied instrument or voice try identifying the materials you are studying and see how they work in that piece; practice the rhythmic reading and sight singing techniques on all your music that you are performing. As you do these activities, you will start to see the music with a greater depth and clarity, and in doing so, bring more to your performances, discussions, and future musical studies.

Robert J. Frank and Kenneth Metz

CD-ROM information

MINIMUM SYSTEM REQUIREMENTS

Macintosh®, Windows® with CD-ROM drive and audio playback

1024 by 768 display

Internet browser (Internet Explorer 6, Firefox, Safari)

Quicktime® recommended

Available hard disc space: 225 MB

INSTALLATION

1   Copy the folder "FFAS" to your hard drive.
2   Open the copy of "FFAS" on your hard drive.
3   Double click on the file "FFAS.html".

For technical inquiries: Contact Robert J. Frank, robfrank@smu.edu.

Acknowledgments

Bringing a regular book to press is in itself a monumental task, but devising, developing, and releasing an interactive hypertext plus hard copy edition magnifies that effort and vision by an exponential magnitude. We wish to thank our editor at Routledge, Constance Ditzel, who recognized our vision and was able to so strongly support it, and to Routledge for taking on the task of approaching a textbook from a new publishing perspective. We also wish to thank Denny Tek, Nicole Solano, Mhairi Baxter, Janice Baiton, and all of the team at Routledge, Taylor & Francis, who worked tirelessly and patiently to accommodate our needs beyond the normal, printed book level. Many thanks to Naxos and our musicians who contributed their talents to the creation of the musical examples, including pianists David Sterrett and Jason E. Ballmann, performers Per-Olov Kindgren, Kevin Kunkel, Carlin Ma, Francesco Mastromatteo, Ryan de Ryke, Daniel Schlosberg, and Daniel Stein. We appreciate their professional talents and generous permissions. More thanks are due to, Professors Chris Anderson and C. Michael Hawn of the Perkins School of Theology and Professors David Mancini and Xi, Wang, of the Department of Music Theory and Composition at SMU, plus the many talented SMU students who gave their assistance in recording the various other examples, including Brent Buemi, Andrew Butler, Chris Coltman, Brady Frazier, Charles Maina Karanja, Maria Nina Lacson, Perry Kyle Larson, Trey Pratt, Katy M. Reiswig, Gina Sexton, Mark A. Trautmann, and Bethany Wildes.

We also acknowledge with appreciation the advice and sabbatical leave support from our Deans, José Bowen (Southern Methodist University, Meadows School of the Arts) and Robert Connally (The University of the Incarnate Word), and the assistance of our friends and colleagues, including Deborah Bussineau-King, Edward Pearsall, Ludim Pedroza, and Farhad Moshiri.

Additional thanks and appreciation go out to all of those who provided valuable support and feedback in surveys and reviews, including Matthew BaileyShea, Eastman School of Music; Michael Berry, Texas Tech University; Duncan Cumming, University at Albany; James Demars, Arizona State University; Jean Guerrero, Eastman School of Music; Bryan Haaheim, University of Kansas; David Heuser, University of Texas at San Antonio; James Kinchen, University of Wisconsin, Parkside; Samuel Magrill, University of Central Oklahoma; Elizabeth Marvin, Eastman School of Music; Andrew Mead, University of Michigan; Rebecca Miller, Hampshire College; Seth Monahan, Eastman School of Music; James Reddan, Linn-Benton Community College; Nancy Marie Rogers, Florida State University; Sarah Satterfield, Central Florida Community College; Nico Schuler, Texas State University; C. Scott Smith, Ohio University; Jessica Suchy-Pilalis, SUNY Potsdam; Dariusz Terefenko, Eastman School of Music; Joseph Van Fleet, Eastern Kentucky University; and Charles Wood, University of Montevallo.

In addition to all of the above, we would also like to thank our teachers, students, and friends from whom we have learned invaluable lessons about being a human being in a world where music is a key part of its infinite beauty.

Finally, we are grateful and thankful to our families, who endured our seemingly endless hours in front for the computer and on the phone with each other as we created and collaborated across the miles, and a special thank you to Rob's loving wife, Kathy.

CHAPTER 1

Introduction and Basics

1.1 Introduction

Composer Edgard Varése once defined **music** as "organized sound." While this simple definition is somewhat vague, it certainly is helpful as a starting point because in order to understand music one must understand how it is organized. Music is a living language that has been developed over centuries and continues to be refined and reinvented by composers and musicians today. In various parts of the world, different musical languages and "dialects" are used. However, the music written in Europe during the **common practice period** from about 1650 to 1900 comprises a very large portion of our musical heritage, and includes such famous composers as **Vivaldi**, **Bach**, **Haydn**, **Mozart**, **Beethoven**, **Schubert**, **Chopin**, **Verdi**, and **Brahms**. Most of the popular music of today still uses the syntax and musical "grammar" of that period. This type of music is based on both **acoustic principles** and tradition, constituting what we often refer to as **tonal** music. Just as words function a certain way within a sentence, **chords** and **rhythms** function a special way within tonal music. Even in other types of music—contemporary art, popular, jazz, Asian, Latin American, African, and Native American—a knowledge of the principles used in Western art music can help one to better understand and appreciate the beauty and structure found within each of these musical art forms. So whether you are a performer, composer, or simply a person who likes listening to music, an understanding of how music works is a valuable and essential asset.

Example 1.1 is one example of a passage of music by **Wolfgang Amadeus Mozart** (1756–1791), perhaps one of the most famous of all the composers of the **common practice** period. In this simple piano work, there are examples of many of the traits of common practice music: **triads**, **arpeggiation**, rhythmic **motives**, **scales**, arch **contours**, **phrases**, **dynamics**. As you listen to Example 1.1, see if you can recognize as many of these traits as possible.

No doubt, some of these traits are familiar to you, and with some time you could figure out some of the details. As you progress through this text, these fundamental aspects and techniques will be studied in greater detail and depth, allowing you to more fluently read, perform, and understand the music you are playing and to make more informed musical choices.

Example 1.1
Mozart, Sonata K. 545, Mvt. I, mm. 1–12

1.2 Basics of Sound

There are some basic terms that are used to talk about sound as it pertains to music.

Frequency—this is a term used to refer to the measurement of the speed of a re-occurring cyclical pattern, such as a sound wave. Frequency is measured in the number of **cycles per second** or **Hertz** (abbreviated **Hz**), named after Heinrich Hertz, who first defined it. Example 1–2 shows a graphical representation of a portion of a sound with a **frequency** of 440 **Hz**. Each repeating "bump" in the shape represents one pulse of sound that is created by your speaker as you listen, and represents one cycle. Over one complete second, there would be exactly 440 cycles of this sound wave.

Pitch—this refers to the highness or lowness of a sound which has a specific, single, steady **frequency**. For instance, Example 1.3 consists of three pitches. The first pitch has a frequency of 440 Hz (cycles per second). The second pitch has a higher frequency (660 Hz), and so it is referred to as "higher" than the first. The third pitch sounds "lower" because the frequency (220 Hz) is much lower than the first pitch.

Example 1.2
Graphical representation of an audio frequency (440 Hz)

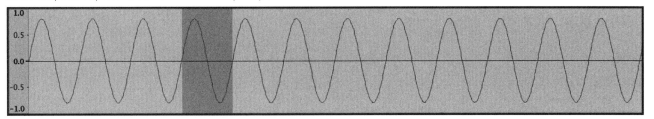

 Example 1.3
Three different pitches

 Example 1.4
Indefinite pitch: Can you sing this pitch? Why or why not?

Rhythm—this is a general term used to refer to when and how long musical sounds occur in time. There will be more discussion about this important term in Chapters 2 and 3 and throughout the text.

 Example 1.5
Rhythmic passage: Play this example several times, try to memorize it and clap along until you can do so accurately.

Timbre (pronounced "TAMber")—this term refers to the "color" or difference in the acoustic wave-shape of a sound. Notice that when different instruments are playing the same **pitches**, only the timbre changes.

 Example 1.6
Different timbres: Can you identify the three instruments in this example by their timbre?

Note—this is the written representation of a given musical **pitch**, **rhythm**, and/or **timbre**. It is also used to refer to the aural sound created when that written note is realized (e.g. "You sang that high note beautifully").

When trying to write down or **notate** these sounds, a system is needed that precisely indicates both the pitch (how high or low the note sounds) and rhythm (how it is played in time). Just as an X–Y graph is used to show these relationships in math, music uses a notation system that notates pitch vertically (higher and lower) and rhythm horizontally (forward in time) as shown in Example 1.7. The following chapters will present how music is notated and read.

 Example 1.7
Pitches notated with different durations

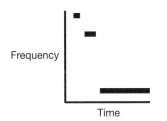

Frequency

Time

Pitch

Rhythm

Dynamics—these are symbols that tell a performer how loud or soft a note should be played. They usually appear below the note that is to be played in instrumental music and above the note in vocal music because the text is placed below the note. Table 1.1 shows some of the most common dynamic markings and their meaning. These terms are in the Italian language because they were developed by Italian composers in the late Renaissance.

Table 1.1 Common Dynamic Markings

Symbol	Italian word	English translation
ppp	pianississimo	very very soft
pp	pianissimo	very soft
p	piano	soft
mp	mezzo-piano	medium soft
mf	mezzo-forte	medium loud
f	forte	loud
ff	fortissimo	very loud
fff	fortississimo	very very loud

Example 1.8

Dynamic markings: Dvorak, Symphony No. 9 "New World", Mvt. II, mm. 1–4

You may also see the terms **crescendo** (*cresc.*) or **diminuendo** (*dim.*) which tell the performer to get louder or softer respectively. These symbols may also be presented as **hairpins** (< for crescendo, and > for diminuendo). Example 1.8 demonstrates many of these symbols.

Chapter Summary

Although there are many different definitions of the term **music**, in general, it is some type of organized sound. Music composed in Europe during the **common practice period** (1600–1900) forms the basis for our traditional system of **notating** music and defining its elements, therefore it is the basis of the study of music fundamentals.

Frequency is the number of cycles per second (or Hertz, abbreviated Hz) of a sound, and a steady, single frequency is called a **pitch**. **Rhythm** is how sounds are arranged in time and the proportional relationships between them. **Timbre** is the acoustic wave-shape that forms the "color" of a pitch. Different instruments will have different timbres or "tone colors." **Dynamics** specify how loud or soft a sound is in musical notation, and are based on Italian terms.

Chapter 1 Exercises

(Audio examples for exercises are included on the CD-ROM)

1   In the following example from the beginning of the chapter (Mozart, Sonata for
Piano K. 545, Mvt. I), listen and follow along with the top part. Discuss in class how
the pitch and rhythm relate to the notation. As the notes get higher, observe how
much they rise in the notation. Follow along several times until you can keep track
of each note both on the page and in the audio example. Make any notes for
in-class discussion below.

_____

_____

_____

Example E1.1

2 Listen to the opening measures of the following works and try to memorize the rhythm. Clap along as a class with the melodies. Are there any patterns you can recognize? Do the pitch patterns always match the rhythmic patterns? Take notes below.

a) Mozart, Symphony No. 40, Mvt. I: 🎵

_____

_____

_____

b) Beethoven, Symphony No. 5, Mvt. I: 🎵

_____

_____

_____

c) Vivaldi, *The Four Seasons*: "Spring", Mvt. I: 🎵

_____

_____

_____

3 What is the overall dynamic for each of the examples in question 2? Do they remain the same, crescendo, or decrescendo? Diagram a rough summary of each below, using the dynamic symbols from Table 1.1 and hairpin crescendos/decrescendos.

a) _____

b) _____

c) _____

4   Are all three examples in question 2 the same timbre? How and when to they vary? What do they all have in common?

_____

_____

_____

_____

_____

_____

_____

5   For each of the following examples of a melody from Schubert's Symphony No. 8 (the "Unfinished" Symphony), identify the name of each instrument by its timbre.

a)   ♪))   _____

b)   ♪))   _____

c)   ♪))   _____

d)   ♪))   _____

e)   ♪))   _____

f)   ♪))   _____

g)   ♪))   _____

h)   ♪))   _____

i)   ♪))   _____

j)   ♪))   _____

Rhythm and Tempo

2.1 The Pulse and the Beat

As mentioned previously, rhythm is a general term used to refer to when and how long musical sounds occur in time. **Rhythm** can be expressed by **notes** with a **pitch**, using an instrument such as a piano, or notes without pitches, using an instrument such as a snare drum. Most **common practice** music contains rhythms that conform to a constant, even **pulse**. This pulse might be fast (over four pulses per second) or slow (less than one pulse per second). We often call this pulse the **beat**. Listen to the following familiar melodies and clap along with the beat.

Example 2.1a and b
Identifying the beat

 2.1a
Mozart, Symphony No. 40, Mvt. I

 2.1b
Identifying the beat
Vivaldi, "Spring" from *The Four Seasons*, Mvt. I

Notice how sometimes you clapped at a moment when there was either a silence or no new note beginning. There were other times when several notes occurred within one beat. Now try to clap the rhythms of the melodies. When rhythm is taught by listening and replicating (as you just did) this is called learning rhythm by **oral tradition**. This method is used in much of the folk music around the world. However, in order to precisely describe in a more consistent and lasting form how musicians need to play notes in time, a system of rhythmic **notation** was developed in Western common practice music that allows composers to write in specific terms how rhythms should be played. When combined with pitch notation, the result is our common practice **musical notation system**.

2.2 Basic Rhythmic Notation

Rhythmic notation is how we specify proportionally where each note begins and ends in relation to the **beat**. Our modern system for notating rhythm has a very logical method of

Example 2.2
Elements of an eighth note

describing how long a note should sound. It uses a set of **noteheads** plus **stems** and **flags** to indicate relative duration (Example 2.2).

A notehead is not a circle: it is an oval that is slanted at about a 30 degree angle upwards. The stem is a very thin, very straight line that goes up or down from the note head, and the flag is a shaped, curved line that is always to the right of the stem. As musical notation is presented, pay particular attention to the details of how the notes are drawn: although many musicians easily read printed music, writing it requires a much more conscious effort to correctly notate it. There is a guide to the process of drawing musical notation, called **musical calligraphy**, in **Appendix 1**.

A **whole note** (see Example 2.3) originally was the standard unit of measure. If it is equally divided into two parts, each of these is called a **half note**. A half note divided into two equal parts yields two **quarter notes**, which are each one quarter of a whole note, hence their name. For each additional subdivision of an **eighth note**, an additional **flag** is added. A **sixteenth note** has two flags, a **thirty-second note** has three flags, and a **sixty-fourth note** has four. Notice how, after the second flag, the length of the **stem** is increased to allow more room for the flags. In common practice music, one rarely encounters a note beyond the sixty-fourth note, but as each note beyond is divided into two parts, the name would double and another flag would be added.

Example 2.3
Standard note values

whole	half	quarter	eighth	sixteenth	thirty-second	sixty-fourth

2.3 Beaming

When a group of notes with **flags** occur within one beat (or in vocal music within one word or syllable), they are **beamed** together to make this grouping more apparent to the performer. The number of beams is equal to the number of flags normally found on the note, so a group of eighth notes has a single beam, a grouping of sixteenth notes has two beams, etc. Beaming does not affect how the music sounds, it is only a notational means of making music easier to read and perform. For example, if the quarter note gets the **beat**, then the beaming of notes should comprise units of quarter notes. Therefore, one would beam two eighth notes together or four sixteenth notes together in order to show the duration equivalent of one quarter note. Example 2.4 shows how flagged notes are beamed together into quarter-note groupings, and also how these notes relate to one another.

Example 2.4
Beaming together of subdivisions and rhythmic proportions

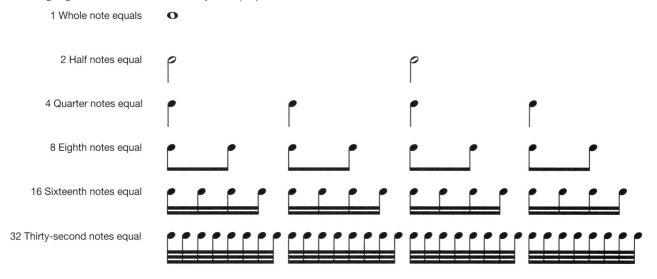

Example 2.5 demonstrates the relationship between these notes in musical notation. This example illustrates how the groupings of notes occur in relation to a given beat value. The beat, in this example a quarter note, determines how notes smaller than a quarter note are beamed together within each beat. The thin, vertical line occurring every four beats is called a **barline**, and each unit between the barlines is called a **measure**. As you listen to Example 2.5, tap along and observe how each measure's notes are half as long (so there are twice as many) as the previous measure's notes. Notice also that the note's value (eighth, sixteenth, etc.) is also that note's proportional relationship to the duration of a whole note. For example, an eighth note lasts 1/8 of a whole note's duration.

Example 2.5
Rhythmic groupings in musical notation

2.4 Rests

Music also requires a method of notating silence. Silence is notated by a **rest**. Rests follow the same hierarchy as **notes**, as the Example 2.6 indicates.

With the exception of the whole and half, rests are generally centered vertically. With whole and half rests, there is an easy way to remember which is which: in a **five-line staff**

Example 2.6
Rests

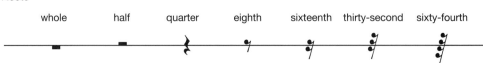

Example 2.7
Whole and half tests in traditional five-line staff notation

whole rests (being larger and therefore "heavier") hang down from the fourth line, and half rests (being smaller) always float above the third line (Example 2.7).

When **beaming** notes together, one does not normally beam over a rest. However, in more contemporary scores, publishers do often include small rests within beamed groups. The following example shows a musical passage first using breaks in the beams and then including rests under beams. Note also that different note values that occur within one **beat** may be beamed together. When beaming notes of mixed values, the number of beams equals the number of **flags** on that note value, and extend throughout all of the notes of that value. In Example 2.8, notice how the sixteenth note beams below only connect adjacent sixteenth notes within each beat, unless "beaming over" rests.

Example 2.8
Two ways of beaming notes and rests

"Breaking" beams over rests

"Beaming over" rests

Notes and rests are spaced horizontally in proportion to their duration, meaning an eighth rest or eighth note will receive the same space, which should be more than a sixteenth note, but less than a quarter note. Spacing within each measure should remain consistent, but may vary between measures according to the content of each. The only exception to this is the whole rest, which when used to fill an empty **measure** is always centered horizontally. Whole notes always occur at the beginning of a measure, as it did in Example 2.5.

2.5 Tied and Dotted Rhythmic Values

There are two methods used to notate more complex values. The first is to use a **tie** to join two note values together into one sustained value. A tie is a curved line connecting the *insides* of two **noteheads** that goes on the opposite side from the stems (Example 2.9). Any two or more note values may be tied together into longer durations, provided a separate tie is used between each notehead. A tie must never extend beyond two noteheads.

Example 2.9
Ties and rhythmic values

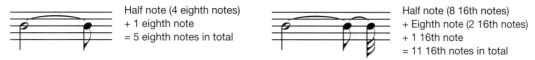

A second method uses a **dot** following the notehead to indicate that the duration is equal to **one and one-half times the note's normal value**. As Example 2.10 demonstrates, a dotted quarter note equals a duration of one quarter (two eighth notes) plus one-half of a quarter note (one eighth note) for a total of three eighth notes duration. A second dot adds half of the first dot's value, or one quarter of the original note's duration, so a **double dotted** quarter note would equal one quarter note (four sixteenth notes) plus an eighth note (two sixteenth notes) plus a sixteenth note for a total of seven sixteenth notes total duration. Any standard note may use a dot or double dot to augment its value. **Triple dotted** notes and beyond are not at all common.

Example 2.10
Dotted note values

2.6 Tuplets

Any standard note value may be divided into any number of equal divisions. When the number of divisions does not equal one of the standard divisions listed earlier (2, 4, 8, etc.), a **tuplet** must be used. A tuplet inserts additional divisions into the normal amount that would be expected for the beat. The exact name of the tuplet depends on the number of divisions it includes. If we wish to have three divisions of a quarter note (instead of the normal two eighth notes), we can use a **triplet** (a three-note tuplet) to accomplish this. Tuplets are notated using the next longest rhythmic value and have a number (with an optional bracket if there is no **beam**) over the grouping. An eighth-note triplet squeezes three eighth notes into the time of two. A **quintuplet** squeezes five notes into the time of four: so if this tuplet occurs over a quarter note beat, you would beam the five notes of the tuplet to match the next larger, normal note value: sixteenth notes (using two beams) as shown in Table 2.1.

When tuplets become too large or cumbersome, they are often broken down into smaller units. For example, a **sextuplet** is frequently broken down into two **triplets**. Notice how at least one beam extends across the entire **beat note**'s duration (in Example 2.11, that being a quarter note).

Larger tuplets (more than eight divisions) are possible and follow the same beaming principles.

Table 2.1 Basic tuplets

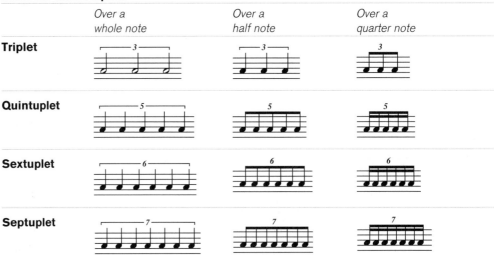

	Over a whole note	Over a half note	Over a quarter note
Triplet			
Quintuplet			
Sextuplet			
Septuplet			

Example 2.11
Common division of larger tuplets

2.7 Tempo

Tempo (plural: **tempi**) is a term used to describe the rate at which beats occur. Tempo is measured in **beats per minute**. Humans, unlike machines, do not have a regular, constant point of reference and cannot accurately and precisely measure tempi "on the spot." Instead, most people will interpret a musical passage at approximately the given tempo. This is acceptable for most **common practice** music, since music is an art which allows for some subjective interpretation in performance and is why most classical music uses only general terms to specify tempo to musicians. However, all aspiring musicians should own and frequently practice with a **metronome** (a device that provides an audio and/or visual signal that indicates precise tempi in beats per minute) to develop a more accurate ability to play at or very near the composer's intended tempo.

Table 2.2 lists a few common terms indicating various tempi. Since Italian was at one time considered the "formal" language for scores in Western music, these Italian terms are still used today, although you may also find tempo markings (also called tempo indications) in English, German, and other languages. While many scores have both the **tempo** marking and a **metronome** marking, some scores may have only one or the other.

Tempo plays an important part in creating the overall character and mood of a piece of music. Listen to the two following examples in Example 2.12 of *The Star Spangled Banner* and note how the mood is affected by the change in tempo:

a) **Examples 2.12a and b**
The Star Spangled Banner at two different tempi

b)

Table 2.2 Examples of common tempo markings

Tempo marking	English translation	Beats per minute	Example
Largo	very slow	40–55	[♪))] Chopin, Prelude, Opus 28, No. 2
Adagio	slow	55–72	[♪))] Chopin, Prelude, Opus 28, No. 4
Andante	moderately slow	72–90	[♪))] Bach, Suite for Cello No. 5 BWV 1011, "Gigue"
Moderato	moderate	90–115	[♪))] Vivaldi, "Spring" from The Four Seasons, Mvt. III
Allegro	fast	115–142	[♪))] Haydn, Piano Sonata XVI-#37, Mvt. I
Presto	very fast	142+	[♪))] Haydn, Piano Sonata XVI-#37, Mvt. III

Chapter Summary

Rhythm is a general term used to refer to when and how long musical sounds occur in time. In the **common practice** system of music, the duration of either a sound or silence is expressed by notational symbols such as a **whole note** or a **half note**. This **rhythmic notation** can represent a specific value relative to the **beat**. Using **ties**, **tuplets**, **dotted values**, and **rests**, any duration of either a sound or a silence can be represented. When rhythms proceed in regular units of time, there is a sense of a **pulse** or **beat**. When notated, notes are often grouped together using **beams** to reflect **beats**. The **tempo** describes the rate at which the beats occur in a piece of music in **beats per minute**. More general **tempo markings** such as *Adagio* or *Presto* are often in the Italian language.

Chapter 2 Exercises

1   Note and Rest Identification, Divisions, and Subdivisions
Draw each of the following, remembering to use a 30 degree inclined oval for the noteheads and properly shaped flags when needed:

a) half note: **b)** eighth note: **c)** whole note:

d) sixteenth note: **e)** quarter rest: **f)** thirty-second note:

g) eighth rest: **h)** half rest: **i)** sixteenth rest:

2   Supply the following information:

a) 1 ♩ = how many ♪s?   _____   **b)** 1 𝅝 = how many ♩s?   _____

c) 3 ♩s = how many ♬s?   _____   **d)** 8 ♬s = how many ♪s?   _____

e) 16 ♬s = how many ♪s?   _____   **f)** 8 ♩s = how many ♪s?   _____

3 Beaming

a) Draw a line to break the beams below to match the requested beat.

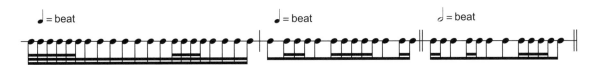

b) Notate the given notes beamed to the given beat value on the staff line below.

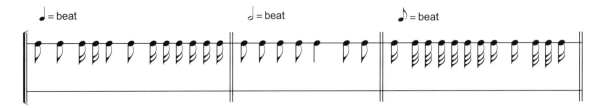

c) Renotate and rebeam the given notes to correctly fit the given beat.

d) Renotate and rebeam the following combinations of notes and rests to fit the given beat.

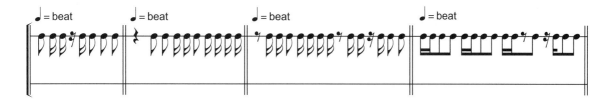

4 Dots and Ties

Notate the following dotted note values as tied standard note values (without dots).

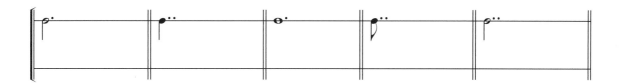

5 Tuplets

Notate the requested tuplet that spans the given note value.

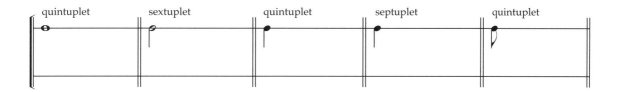

6 Tempo

Listen to the examples on the CD-ROM and provide both the Italian term and your estimate of the number of beats per minute for the tempo of that passage.

a) Tempo marking: _____ beats per minute: _____

b) Tempo marking: _____ beats per minute: _____

c) Tempo marking: _____ beats per minute: _____

d) Tempo marking: _____ beats per minute: _____

e) Tempo marking: _____ beats per minute: _____

f) Tempo marking: _____ beats per minute: _____

g) Tempo marking: _____ beats per minute: _____

h) Tempo marking: _____ beats per minute: _____

i) Tempo marking: _____ beats per minute: _____

j) Tempo marking: _____ beats per minute: _____

CHAPTER 3

Proportional Value, Meter, and Grouping

3.1 Relative Proportional Values of Notes and Rests

The proportional organization of durations is a crucial concept in understanding how **common practice** music unfolds in time. In order to express how long a sound or silence lasts, a point of reference to the pulse or **beat** is needed. The **rhythmic note value** that is assigned to the beat is called the **beat note**. Any note value may assume the value of one beat. Relative values for other notes vary according to which rhythmic duration is assigned the beat. For instance, when the half note is the **beat note** (a value of one beat), the whole note has a relative value of two beats (twice as along) and the quarter note has the value ½ beat (see the third column of Table 3.1). This table demonstrates how relative note values depend on which note is the **beat note**. Notice that the first column clearly shows how the half, quarter, eighth, and sixteenth notes got their names, relative to the whole note.

Table 3.1 Rhythmic proportions

| Beat note: → | Value (in beats) relative to the beat note | | | | |
	𝅝	𝅗𝅥	𝅘𝅥	𝅘𝅥𝅮	𝅘𝅥𝅯
𝅝	1	2	4	8	16
𝅗𝅥	½	1	2	4	8
𝅘𝅥	¼	½	1	2	4
𝅘𝅥𝅮	⅛	¼	½	1	2
𝅘𝅥𝅯	1⁄16	⅛	¼	½	1

3.2 Proportionate Division and Subdivision in Musical Performance

In order for a performer to accurately realize **rhythm**, a clear understanding of these proportions is essential. Music is a temporal art and so, on many different levels, time plays a vital role in the very existence of music. In Western thought, time is considered to be capable of **division** into segments of equal value, a concept that led to the invention of the clock (where days divide into hours, which divide into minutes, which divide into seconds). The term **divisive rhythm** describes how rhythm in **common practice** music is conceived of and notated. To demonstrate this, listen to Example 3.1 and clap along with the beat. As you clap, count along with the music naturally, as you feel it. Don't stop—keep counting all the way to the end.

 **Example 3.1**
Divisive rhythm

Did you keep counting to some larger number or did you automatically break it down into smaller groupings of maybe two or four **beats**? If you did, then that is an example of divisive rhythm. Most people will commonly break long strings of data (numbers, beats, etc.) into smaller divisions of groups of two, three, four, or sometimes five. However, even groups of four can be divided into two groups of two, and five can be divided into a group of two and a group of three. Think of a phone number, social security number, zip code, or other such string of numbers, and notice how they are naturally broken into these smaller divisions.

Musicians are humans and not machines. It is much easier to keep track of time when it is broken down into smaller units, and when longer durations are related proportionately to those smaller units. This is the skill that allows musicians to perform rhythms more accurately and to keep a steady **tempo** over longer periods of time. Conductors also lead via proportional movements based on beats and groupings, since conducting each and every note is usually physically impossible.

3.3 Simple and Compound Groupings and Meter

As noted above, the most basic patterns comprise groups of two or three equal-valued notes. Groupings of two notes are referred to as **simple groupings**, and **compound groupings** refer to groupings of three. As you may have noticed in the previous examples, there is a natural emphasis (called an **accent**) placed on the first beat of each group. In the Western system of music notation, **meter** creates groupings of pulses into recurring patterns of strong (S), accented **beats** and/or weak (w), unaccented beats.

SIMPLE Groupings						**COMPOUND Groupings**								
S	w	S	w	S	w	S	w	w	S	w	w	S	w	w
1	2	1	2	1	2	1	2	3	1	2	3	1	2	3

All larger patterns are generally perceived according to these two basic grouping types. For example, in music which has a four-beat pattern, these four beats can be divided at a higher level into two simple groups of two beats. When this happens, beat three is not as strong as beat one since at a higher level it is a weak beat. This is most obvious at slower tempi:

Higher Level		S		w		S		w		etc.
Lower Level		S	w	S	w	S	w	S	w	etc.
		1	2	3	4	1	2	3	4	

In the same way a group of six beats can be reduced to three simple (two) groups that function as a compound grouping at a higher level:

Higher Level		S		w		w			
Lower Level		S	w	S	w	S	w		
		1	2	3	4	5	6		

Or, with a different combination of strong and weak beats, the same group of six beats can be reduced to two compound (three) groups that function as a simple grouping at a higher level:

Higher Level		S			w				
Lower Level		S	w	w	S	w	w		
		1	2	3	4	5	6		

The only difference between each of the two previous six-beat groupings is in how they are organized and **accented**.

This hierarchical structure of simple (two) or compound (three) beats in common practice music is called **meter**. In musical notation, this is indicated by a **time signature**, which provides information on how many notes are in each **measure** and how they are grouped. A time signature (Example 3.2) is notated by two numbers, one above the other, at the beginning of each piece and whenever there is a change of meter in the work.

Example 3.2
Meter and time signature: Mozart, Clarinet Concerto in A major K. 622, mm. 57–65

Each **measure** is separated on the page by a **barline**. The first beat of each measure is called the **downbeat**. The last beat of each measure is commonly called the **upbeat**. These terms derive from the way conductors move their arms to indicate the beats. The following are **conducting patterns** for the three most common number of beats in common practice music: two-, three- and four-beat measures (called **duple**, **triple**, and **quadruple**, respectively). Solid lines show the basic pattern, and dotted lines indicate the movement of the right hand (facing the page).

Example 3.3
Basic conducting patterns for the three basic meter types

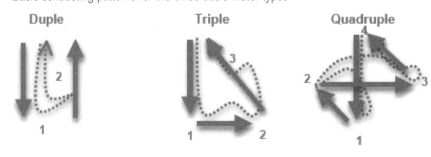

PROPORTIONAL VALUE, METER, AND GROUPING

3.4 Simple Meter

In **simple meter**, each beat divides into **simple groupings** (two equal parts) and the **beat note** is always a standard note type (quarter note, half note, eight note, etc.).

In simple meter time signatures:

> **The top number indicates the number of beats per measure.**
> **The bottom number indicates the beat note type.**

If there is a "4" in the lower number, the quarter note receives the beat. A "2" would indicate that the half note would receive the beat, a "16" would indicate a sixteenth note receiving the beat, etc. In this manner, the lower number functions similar to the fractions in column one of **Table 3.1**. The top number indicates the number of beats the measure contains, which in common practice music is typically either two, three, or four beats. Table 3.2 lists the most common simple meters.

Table 3.2 Simple meter

Type of simple meter	Beat note type	Divided beat type	Time signature
Duple	Half note	Quarter note	$\frac{2}{2}$ or ¢
Duple	Quarter note	Eighth note	$\frac{2}{4}$
Duple	Eighth note	Sixteenth note	$\frac{2}{8}$
Triple	Half note	Quarter note	$\frac{3}{2}$
Triple	Quarter note	Eighth note	$\frac{3}{4}$
Triple	Eighth note	Sixteenth note	$\frac{3}{8}$
Quadruple	Half note	Quarter note	$\frac{4}{2}$
Quadruple	Quarter note	Eighth note	$\frac{4}{4}$ or **C**
Quadruple	Eighth note	Sixteenth note	$\frac{4}{8}$

The time signature of $\frac{4}{4}$ may also appear as **C** (for **common time**). One may also find a "C" with a slash through it (¢) indicating **cut time** which is equal to $\frac{2}{2}$.

3.5 Proportion in Simple Meters

One function of a **time signature** is to set the value of a specific rhythmic duration to the value of one **beat**. Another function is to indicate the number of beats in the **measure**. Although these numbers and **beat note** types will change, there is one important principle that remains the same: the proportional relationship discussed in the **beginning of this chapter**.

Notice that although in $\frac{4}{4}$ the quarter note is the **beat note** type and gets one beat, proportional relationship remains the same between all note values:

♩ is still ¼ of a 𝅝   ♩ is still ½ of a 𝅗𝅥, etc.

However, because the quarter note is now the **beat note** type, the whole note now has a value of four beats. Often beginning musicians think of rhythmic proportions only as fractions of a beat (i.e. ¼ of a beat), but the larger proportions (4:1) are just as important. This is an often-overlooked requirement for understanding how Western music describes durations of sounds and rests. Almost any duration of a sound or rest can be expressed as a number, fraction, or mixed number value. Only the **beat note** type changes depending on the **time signature**, which sets a specific note type to the value of one **beat**. All proportions remain the same, regardless of the time signature or **tempo**.

3.6 Compound Meter

Compound meter is used to notate music that has **compound groupings** (three **divisions** per beat: S w w). The most common forms are **duple**, **triple**, or **quadruple**. Example 3.4 is from the music of **Beethoven** and provides an instance of compound meter.

Example 3.4
Compound meter: Beethoven, Sonatina in G major, Mvt. II

You may notice that Example 3.4 begins with an incomplete **measure** consisting of only three eighth notes on the **upbeat**. Melodies that begin with incomplete measures are quite common and these will be discussed in more detail in section **3.10**. Most people will hear the complete measures in this example in terms of two-beat groupings with three divisions per beat. Listen again, counting a fast "1—2—3—2—2—3 . . . 1—2—3—2—2—3 . . ." accenting the strong beats.

In compound meter, each beat is divided into three equal, standard note types. Because three of any standard note type (eighth, quarter, half, etc.) will equal a **dotted** note value, the note receiving the beat will always be *a dotted note value* (i.e. a dotted quarter, a dotted half, a dotted eight, etc.).

Example 3.5
Dotted beat values in compound meters

Since time signatures may only use whole numbers for their values, and compound meters use dotted values for the beat note type (1½ of a standard note value), they require a slightly different approach to how their time signatures are constructed. Unlike simple meter, the top numbers in a compound meter **time signature** indicate the number of *divided* beat notes per measure, not the number of beats. In compound meter, the division is always by three, so the top number for compound time signatures will always be a multiple of three. The most common top numbers for compound time signatures are: 6 for compound **duple** (2 beats × 3 divisions = 6), 9 for compound **triple** (3 beats × 3 divisions = 9), or 12 for compound **quadruple** (4 beats × 3 divisions = 12). The bottom number in a compound time signature is also constructed differently from that of a simple time signature: the bottom number in a compound time signature indicates the rhythmic note value that receives the *divided* beat.

In compound meter time signatures:

The top number indicates the number of divided beat notes per measure.
The bottom number indicates the divided beat note type.

Because of this, in compound meter, the number of actual beats per measure is the top number divided by three. So a "6" in the top number means that there are "six divided by three" beats, or two beats per measure. Rarely, and only in very slow passages, the divided beat is sometimes heard as the beat. Although you may hear the divided note value as "the beat," in notation the **beaming** of such passages still reflects **compound grouping** typical of any compound meter.

Table 3.3 Compound meter

Type of simple meter	Beat note type	Divided beat type	Time signature
Duple	Dotted half note	Quarter note	$\frac{6}{4}$
Duple	Dotted quarter note	Eighth note	$\frac{6}{8}$
Duple	Dotted eighth note	Sixteenth note	$\frac{6}{16}$
Triple	Dotted half note	Quarter note	$\frac{9}{4}$
Triple	Dotted quarter note	Eighth note	$\frac{9}{8}$
Triple	Dotted eighth note	Sixteenth note	$\frac{9}{16}$
Quadruple	Dotted half note	Quarter note	$\frac{12}{4}$
Quadruple	Dotted quarter note	Eighth note	$\frac{12}{8}$
Quadruple	Dotted eighth note	Sixteenth note	$\frac{12}{16}$

3.7 Beaming in Simple and Compound Meters

When **beaming** eighth notes and smaller values in both **simple** and **compound** meters, it is important to beam within the **beat**. This not only allows the performer to properly count the passage, but also indicates where the strong and weak beats occur. Consider the excerpt from **Bach**'s Suite No. 1 for 'Cello in Example 3.6. It is written in $\frac{6}{8}$ (compound-duple) and is notated as follows:

Example 3.6
Compound meter in Bach, Suite No. 1 for 'Cello

Now notice how it changes if it is rewritten into $\frac{3}{4}$ (triple-simple) meter and rebeamed:

Example 3.7
Bach, Suite No. 1 transcribed into simple–triple time

Although the notes and rhythmic durations are the same, the meaning of the music via the change of strong and weak **accents** is completely changed.

3.8 Tuplets in Compound Meter

Since the **beat note** divides into three, not two, equal parts in **compound** meter, two and four note divisions are now non-standard and must be **notated** as a **tuplet**. When composers wish to use one of these divisions of the beat, a **duplet** or **quadruplet**, respectively, is used. The method of determining the number of **beams** for compound meters is slightly different from the method used for **simple** meters. In compound meter, the number of beams is equal to the *non-dotted*, simple meter counterpart: so for a two-note division of a dotted quarter-note beat, a non-dotted quarter note would divide into two eighth notes, and the duplet would have one beam (eighth notes) with a "2" outside of the beam. A quadruplet over a dotted quarter note would have two beams, just as would four sixteenth notes occurring over a non-dotted quarter note.

Example 3.8

Two examples of duplets and quadruplets in compound meters

3.9 Summary of Common Meter Types

Important hint: to keep the difference between simple and compound meter straight, remember:

SIMPLE MEANS "KEEP IT SIMPLE"

In simple meter, the top number is the number of beats in each measure and the bottom number is the **beat note** value.

COMPOUND MEANS DIVIDED (BY THREE)

In compound meter, the top number is the number of *divided (by three)* beat notes per measure and the bottom number is the *divided (by three)* **beat note** value. The beat itself will be a dotted note value three times larger than the divided **beat note** value.

Table 3.4 Summary of metric types

	Simple	Compound
Duple	$\frac{2}{2}$, $\frac{2}{4}$, $\frac{2}{8}$, $\frac{2}{16}$, etc. Simple-Duple or "SD"	$\frac{6}{4}$, $\frac{6}{8}$, $\frac{6}{16}$, etc. Compound-Duple or "CD"
Triple	$\frac{3}{2}$, $\frac{3}{4}$, $\frac{3}{8}$, $\frac{3}{16}$, etc. Simple-Triple or "ST"	$\frac{9}{4}$, $\frac{9}{8}$, $\frac{9}{16}$, etc. Compound-Triple or "CT"
Quadruple	$\frac{4}{2}$, $\frac{4}{4}$, $\frac{4}{8}$, $\frac{4}{16}$, etc. Simple-Quadruple or "SQ"	$\frac{12}{4}$, $\frac{12}{8}$, $\frac{12}{16}$, etc. Compound-Quadruple or "CQ"

3.10 Non-metered Music and the Anacrusis

Most of the music of the **common practice period** conforms to one of the time signatures described in this chapter. However, there are exceptions, such as when a composer notates a **cadenza**, which is a free, non-metered solo of any length which may or may not use clear, consistent beats. Example 3.9 shows the use of a **fermata** (⌢) to indicate that the pulse stops and all parts must wait until the oboe finishes its cadenza.

Example 3.9
Beethoven, Symphony No. 5, mvt. I, oboe cadenza

As seen earlier in this chapter, sometimes composers will use an incomplete measure called an **anacrusis** containing what are often informally called "pick up" notes. When this occurs, the last measure of the piece is usually reduced by the total rhythmic value of the anacrusis so that the entire piece has a full number of beats that matches the meter(s) employed, as in Example 3.10.

Example 3.10
The anacrusis

3.11 Advanced Topics: Asymmetrical and Mixed Meter

Modern composers and many styles of folk music have frequently made use of meters that have a mixed combination of **simple** and **compound** groupings as part of the grouping pattern within one measure. For example |SwSww| or |SwwSw| would be a pattern for the meter that would have 5 as its top number. Because of the unequal length of the beats, these types of meters are called **asymmetrical meters**. In order to determine the beat groupings in asymmetrical meters, one must pay careful attention to the beams indicated in the music, as Example 3.11 illustrates. Notice that, as in this example, the meter may change in any measure in the middle of a work. The new **time signature** remains in effect until the end of the piece or another time signature occurs. This technique is called **mixed meter**.

Example 3.11
Asymmetrical and mixed meters

Chapter Summary

The notation of Western **common practice** music relies on the concept of **divisive rhythm** in order to create **notational** symbols that specify durations which are in proportional relationship to each other. The **beat note** is any note value that is assigned the value of one beat, and although the relative value of the other notes depends on this assignment, the proportional relationship between them does not change. **Meter** is the hierarchical organization of **beats** and **divisions**. Meter organizes recurring patterns of strong and weak beats into units called **measures**. Simple meters are based on **simple groupings** (S-w) at the divided level. Compound meters are based on **compound groupings** (S-w-w) at the divided level. Most meters are **duple** (two beats per measure), **triple** (three beats per measure), or **quadruple** (four beats per measure). Other meters that contain a mixture of simple and compound groupings, or an odd number of beats in a measure, are termed **asymmetric** types. Meters are indicated by use of a **time signature**, which specifies the organization and hierarchy of beats in each measure. Time signatures for simple meters are constructed with the number of beats as the top number and the beat note value as the lower number. Time signatures for compound meters are constructed with the number of divided beats as the top number and the divided beat note value as the lower number. **Beaming** of notes with **flags** must occur only within the **beat note** value. Time signatures remain in effect throughout a work or until a new time signature is specified. Works making use of frequently changing time signatures are said to be in **mixed meter**. Non-metric passages may be found in some pieces, for example in a **cadenza**. Some passages begin with an incomplete measure called an **anacrusis**, also known informally as a "pick up" note or measure.

Chapter 3 Exercises

1 Fill in the numeric value that each of the following notes represents relative to the given beat note value:

a) Beat note value = ♩.

𝅝 = 2   ♪ = _____   ♩. = _____   𝅗𝅥＿♩. = _____

b) Beat note value = 𝅗𝅥

♪ = _____   𝅝＿𝅘𝅥𝅘𝅥 = _____   𝅗𝅥.. = _____   𝅘𝅥𝅘𝅥♪. = _____

c) Beat note value = ♪

𝅝 = _____   𝅘𝅥𝅮. = _____   𝅘𝅥.＿𝅘𝅥 = _____   𝅘𝅥＿𝅘𝅥♪. = _____

2 Using the quarter note as the beat note value, notate the following number of beats using the fewest possible rest symbols:

Example: 9 = ▬   ▬   𝄽

a) 7 =   **b)** 9 ¾ =   **c)** 5 ⅛ =

d) 12 ⅜ =   **e)** 3 ⁵⁄₁₆ =   **f)** 3 ¾ =

3 Listen to the audio examples on the CD-ROM, and identify each as either simple (S) or compound (C) groupings (circle the correct answer):

a) S C   **b)** S C   **c)** S C   **d)** S C   **e)** S C

4 Identify each of the following as simple (S) or compound (C) groupings:

a) ____

b) ____

c) ____

d) ____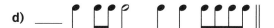

5 Write the beat note value for the following time signatures:

a) $\frac{3}{2}$ _____   **b)** $\frac{6}{8}$ _____   **c)** $\frac{9}{32}$ _____   **d)** $\frac{3}{4}$ _____   **e)** $\frac{6}{4}$ _____

6 Complete the following table. The first row has been completed for you.

Simple (S) or Compound(C)	Duple(D), Triple(T), or Quadruple (Q)	Beat Note Type	Divided Beat Type	Time Signature
S	Q	Quarter Note	Eighth Note	$\mathbf{C}$ or $\frac{4}{4}$
				$\frac{9}{8}$
S	Q		Sixteenth Note	
C	T	Dotted Half Note		
C	D		Eighth Note	
S	T		Sixteenth Note	
				$\frac{12}{32}$
S	Q		Thirtysecond Note	
		Dotted Half Note		Top Number 12
	T	Dotted Quarter Note		8 Bottom Number

7 Add time signatures as needed to the following passage:

8 Rewrite the following passages to create the correct beaming and grouping. The first example contains an anacrusis. Add rests to complete each final measure.

a)

b)

9 Compose and properly notate an interesting rhythmic passage that you are able to perform. Make it eight measures long in either compound-duple or simple-triple time.

Aural Application

Rhythmic Reading and Metric Transcription

Although music simultaneously combines basic elements such as rhythm, pitch, dynamics, and timbre, in order to master each element it is useful to study them separately. Rhythm is primary to a study of all the other elements, as music exists only in time. An understanding of rhythm needs to include a method to read and count various rhythms notated in any meter. **Rhythmic reading** is a method used by many musicians to become fluent and proficient at mastering rhythm and meter, and to communicate with one another about the rhythmic elements of music. Although the process presented in this single chapter is simple and easy to understand, like so many aspects of music, it will no doubt take regular practice over a longer period of time to become fluent in it. As musical passages are studied in each future chapter, this process should be applied to reading them as well as the other music that you read on a daily basis until it becomes thoroughly internalized and mastered.

Chapter 3 presented the fundamentals of **meter**, and rhythmic reading is directly derived from the way meter functions. The first aspect is the identification of the **beat note** value, then defining the **division** and **subdivisions** of the beat. Since there are two types of beat groupings, **simple groupings** for **simple meters**, and **compound groupings** for **compound meters**, these will be covered separately. Regardless of whether a musical passage is in simple or compound meter, the beat note value governs the approach to reading the rhythm.

4.1 Rhythmic Reading in Simple Meter

In any given meter, there is a beat note value and the number of beats per measure. Rhythmic reading is based on the **beat count** and how that beat count number divides and subdivides. For example, in $\frac{4}{4}$ there are four beats per measure and the quarter note gets the beat. One counts these beats according to the time signature as shown in Example 4.1. The same metric **accents** are placed on the **downbeat** and weaker beats, as discussed in **Chapter 3**.

Example 4.1
Beat count

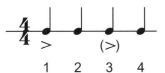

Each beat may divide and subdivide. There are several systems in use that assign various syllables to the divisions and subdivision, and each has its merits and problems. The system in use by many professional musicians and in this text employs a method of rhythmic reading based on counting beats with numbers. For simple groupings, the syllable "and" (notated with the symbol "&") is used for the division of a beat, and the syllables "e" (pronounced "ee"—long "e") for the first subdivision and "a" (pronounced "ah"—short "a") for the final subdivision. Table 4.1 shows how a single beat divides and subdivides for typical, simple meters.

Notice how the beat and divided beat syllable remains the same regardless of whether it is subdivided or not. This allows for the principle of **subdivision** throughout an entire passage as a means of keeping a steady, accurate tempo. Even when reading longer note values, if one is silently dividing or subdividing the beat into the smallest note value present in the passage, the resulting reading will be more accurate.

**Table 4.1 Divisions and subdivisions of the beat in rhythmic reading for simple
             meters**

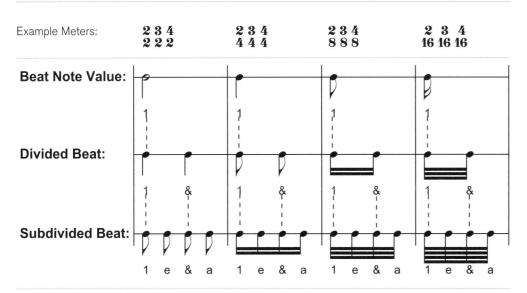

For example, if reading the rhythm in Example 4.2, each note is read using the syllable on which it begins, then sustained throughout the length of that note's value. Notice how every syllable matches perfectly with the division notated above it.

This principle of division and subdivision is based upon the same principle as measuring time in general: if there is only an hour hand (beat) on your watch, you will not be able to accurately measure time intervals less than an hour. If there is both an hour and a minute

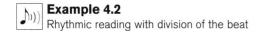

Example 4.2
Rhythmic reading with division of the beat

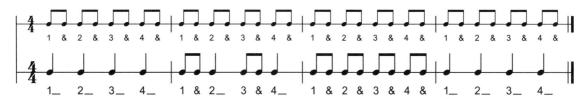

hand on your watch, you can measure time accurately down to the minute (division), which may be good enough for some applications, but not if events are proceeding at smaller intervals. This is why precision stopwatches used for measuring critical times in sporting events such as race car driving or Olympic swimming and track measure time down to very small intervals (subdivisions). When the difference in time between events is only a few milliseconds apart, that smallest difference is the value at which the division of time must be measured. In music, this can be translated to the following principle which governs accurate rhythmic reading:

> **Whatever the smallest rhythmic note value is for a given passage, that is the division or subdivision that should be used for the entire passage.**

Using this principle, all longer note values will be accurately in proportion to the shorter note values. As seen in the **previous chapter on rhythm and proportion**, this is one of the most important elements of Western music. This is essential for the ability to read note values longer than the **beat note** value. The same principle covers all durational values within a **simple grouping** system. **Dotted** and **tied** note values simply sustain the syllable upon which they began for the entire duration of the note value. However, for these values, it is even more important to mentally subdivide to the smallest note value to ensure a correct duration. Example 4.3 demonstrates the silent, mental divisions or subdivisions (shown in parenthesis) needed in order to accurately perform the passages. Although only

Example 4.3
Subdivision and dotted or tied note values

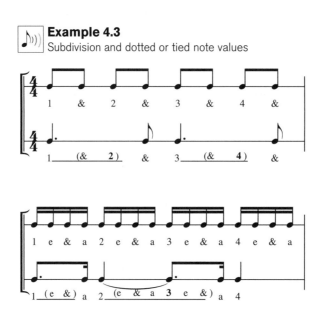

the starting syllable is spoken and sustained out loud, these mental time markers should be forcefully and evenly counted internally, accenting the beat note numbers. Notice how with these internal reference points, the location of the notes following the dotted and tied values is absolutely clear and precise.

In Example 4.4, the shortest rhythmic value is a sixteenth note, which is the subdivision of the quarter-note beat, hence this is the value to which the *entire* passage must be subdivided in order to accurately perform it. To demonstrate this, try reading this example as a class at a moderate **tempo** of about 60 beats per minute, first *without* the subdivisions, then with half of the class counting the subdivisions and the other half reading the rhythm below it.

Example 4.4
Subdivision and longer note values

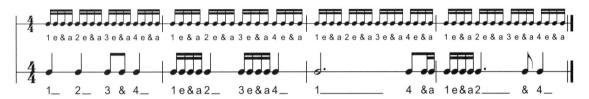

You probably found that without the subdivisions the class was together during the first two **measures**, but after the longer note values, it was harder to all come in together. This reinforces a basic rhythmic principle that is overlooked by many aspiring musicians, but is essential for accurate performance: **the longer the note value, the more important the subdivision becomes.**

Rests are read as silence, just as in musical performance. Notes preceding the rest should be held to their full value, and to ensure accuracy the silent, mental subdivision should continue throughout the rest.

In all simple meters, regardless of type, the same principle applies. Beats are counted with an **accent** on the **downbeat**, notes are spoken on the syllable on which they begin and sustained throughout the duration of that note, and rests are silent. Example 4.5 contains examples of how various passages in different meters would be read.

Example 4.5
Simple meter rhythmic reading examples

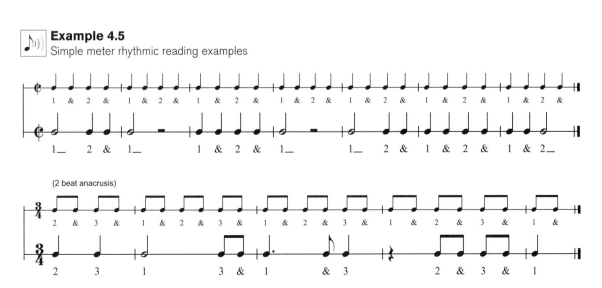

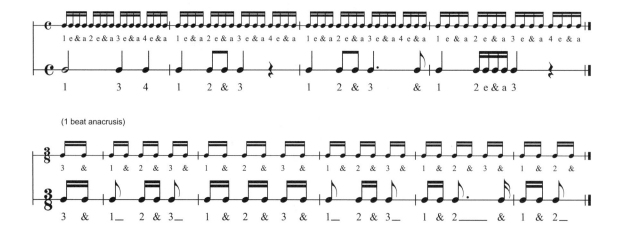

4.2 Rhythmic Reading in Compound Meter

Since **compound meters** use three-note **compound groupings**, a different method of dividing the beat is needed. One popular method taught in elementary schools uses the syllables "la li" for the divisions of the beat. However, the following system is used by many professional conductors and musicians in their daily music making, and therefore is the system that will be used in this text. The **beat note** value is still read as the beat count, just as in simple meter. In compound meters, the beat note value will always be a **dotted** note value. Since there are three divisions of the beat, the first division is read as the beat count, the second as a softer "2" and the third as a softer "3." Then, subdivisions are read as "and" (&) just as divisions are in simple meter. This system is based on how compound time signatures are constructed: since the lower number is the divided beat note value, this is the note value divided by "&." Since all subdivisions of this divided beat note value subdivide in the same manner as simple meters (into two parts) each subdivision can be further subdivided in the slow tempi in the same manner as simple meters using this method. Table 4.2 lists the beat note with its division and subdivision for commonly found compound meters in both systems.

Table 4.2 Divisions and subdivisions of the beat in rhythmic reading for compound meters

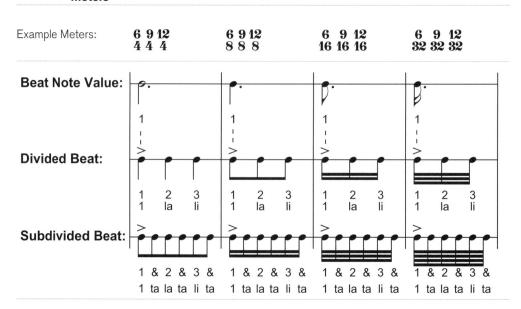

The principles for rhythmic reading in simple meters still apply. Beats are counted with an **accent** on the **downbeat** and a lesser accent on each subsequent beat. Notes are spoken on the syllable on which they begin and sustained throughout the duration of that note, and rests are silent. Passages should always be divided or subdivided to the smallest rhythmic value used within the passage.

If your class uses the "la li" method, divided beats would be read "1 la li" and subdivided beats read "1 ta la ta li ta." Each subsequent beat still begins with the beat number.

Example 4.6 contains examples of how various passages in compound meters would be read.

Example 4.6
Compound meter rhythmic reading examples

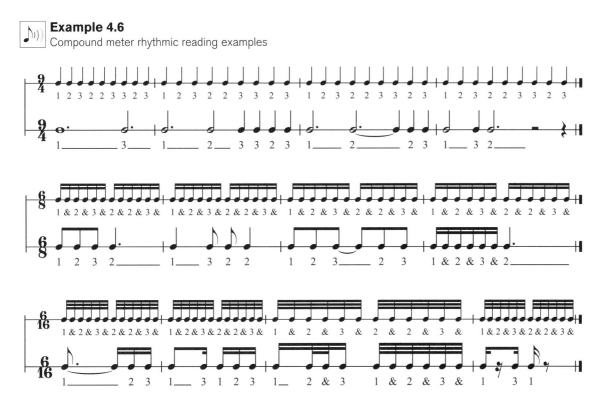

4.3 Reading Tuplets within Simple Groupings

Tuplets are divisions of a note value into a non-standard number of parts. When reading tuplets within **simple groupings**, each tuplet division is read as a number corresponding to the number of divisions contained in the tuplet (see Example 4.7). For example, a triplet has three divisions, so it would be read beginning with the beat count, and the "2 3." A quintuplet, with five divisions of the beat, would begin with the beat count then "2 3 4 5." Like compound meter reading, this allows for further subdivision using "&" if needed.

Example 4.7
Tuplets within simple groupings

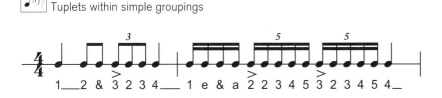

Because the division of the beat is changing and not consistent, the silent, mental subdivision of the beat should continue only within passages without tuplets. When the passage with the tuplets is over, normal subdivision should resume.

Although the principle is simple, accurate performance of tuplets requires diligent practice until one is able to accurately and smoothly change between any division of the beat—standard or tuplet. This brief introduction should be reinforced throughout your musical studies.

4.4 Reading Tuplets within Compound Groupings

The only **tuplets** normally occurring in **compound groupings** are **duplets** and **quadruplets**. As these sound in performance exactly like the standard division and subdivision of the beat in simple meters, the same set of syllables is used as in simple meter, as seen in Example 4.8. As with simple meter, when the passage containing the tuplets is completed, normal mental, silent subdivision should resume.

Example 4.8

Example 4.8: Tuplets within compound groupings

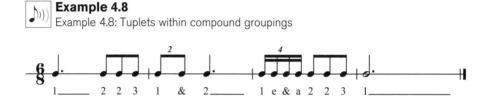

4.5 Metric Transcription

You may have noted that in Table 4.1, the beat, division, and subdivision was read using the same syllables regardless of the duration of the **beat note** value. As you listen to Example 4.9, can you tell only by the recording which of the two examples is being played?

Example 4.9

Main theme, Haydn, Trumpet Concerto in E-flat, Mvt. I

In fact, there is no difference between how either of these two examples would sound because all of the durations and tempo are proportionally equivalent. The only difference is in the notation. In the second example, the lower number in the time signature is changed from a quarter note (4) to an eighth note (8) and all of the note values are one half of the duration of those in the first example. This process is called **metric transcription**.

Metric transcription in simple meter involves re-notating a passage of music from one **meter** into another whose **beat note value** is either larger or smaller depending upon the new *bottom* number in the time signature. The *top* number (the number of beats in the measure) does not change. All of the rhythmic note values are scaled proportionate to the **beat note** value's change in duration. If the beat note value doubles, then all note values must double. If the beat note value is reduced to a quarter of the previous beat note's value, then all notes must be reduced to a quarter their previous duration. If the same **tempo** is used for the beat note value, the passage should sound exactly the same because all of the basic rhythmic relationships do not change.

Notice how rhythmic transcription can help make the notation of a passage appear simpler. Example 4.10 increases or **augments** the values proportionally, creating an easier-to-read passage that will sound exactly the same as the original.

Example 4.10
Simplifying a passage via rhythmic transcription

Rhythmic transcription can be used for practical purposes to arrange more complicated passages into a simpler written form for younger musicians. This is a common technique in creating middle school arrangements. Some musicians also find it helpful to "mentally transcribe" passages into a simpler meter when working out difficult passages. Either way, rhythmic transcription is a powerful and helpful tool for all musicians.

4.6 Metric Transcription between Simple and Compound Meters

Sometimes composers notate music in a **simple meter** that could easily transcribe metrically to **compound meter**. This is especially evident if the passage contains many triplets in succession. Example 4.11 is a voice with piano reduction of the orchestral score from the opera *Rigoletto* by **Giuseppe Verdi**. It is notated in **common time**, but may well have been done in **quadruple-compound meter**. In this example, only the first measure shows the eighth note triplet values that continue in the left hand part, assuming the musician will recognize this pattern.

This passage could easily be transcribed into $\frac{12}{8}$ since there are four beats, each with a three-note division of the beat. Only in the fourth measure does the melody slip briefly into a two-note division of the beat. In either case, the resulting sound would be the same, and so it simply becomes a matter of preference for the composer as to which version is used.

Example 4.11
Metric transcription of Verdi, *Rigoletto*, Act II, No. 14

Original:

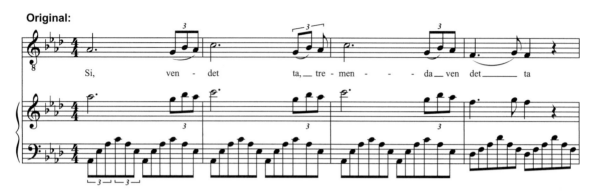

Metric transcription:

Franz Schubert used a combination of both simple and compound meter in his Opus 24 No. 1 (Example 4.12), where the vocal part is notated in **common time** (quadruple-simple) and the piano accompaniment is notated in $\frac{12}{8}$ (quadruple-compound). Notice that although the voice and piano have different **beat note** values, the tempo of the beats is identical. Since the piano has no **simple groupings** and the voice has no **compound groupings**, this allows Schubert to create an easier part for each to perform without the need of a single tuplet. This technique, where two meters are used simultaneously, is called **polymeter** and is normally found only in music of the twentieth century. This does, however, demonstrate that composers of the **common practice** period often thought about and used the interesting juxtaposition of simple against compound groupings in their music.

4.7 Rhythmic Reduction

Besides reading rhythms, the study of rhythm applies to analyzing music in rhythmic and metrical dimensions. One may take a passage of music and analyze only the rhythm. This task is often begun by creating a **rhythmic reduction**. In Mozart's Symphony No. 40, Mvt. I, the melody of the opening nine measures could be rhythmically reduced as shown in Example 4.13.

This reduction uses **rhythmic notation**, in which the **noteheads** are not the normal, 30 degree ovals, but instead are 45 degree slashes, (or other shapes, such as an "x") on a one-lined **staff**. This indicates that the reduction does not specify a pitch. As you read this

Example 4.12
Schubert, Opus 24, No. 1

Example 4.13
Rhythmic reduction of: Mozart, Symphony No. 40, Mvt. I, mm. 1–9

rhythmic reduction, you may notice the passage contains a repeating rhythmic pattern, shown under the brackets. This is an example of a **rhythmic motive**. Composers frequently make use of rhythmic motives—some very short and simple, some longer like this—to provide an element of unity and organization to the music. Creating a rhythmic reduction often helps reveal these more clearly.

Chapter Summary

Rhythmic reading is a means of accurately realizing and communicating about rhythm. Beats are counted and syllables are assigned to the divisions and subdivisions of the beat. By silently referencing a continuous **division** or **subdivision** of the beat equal to the smallest rhythmic value used in the passage, the proportion of all note values will be more accurate. The longer the note values are in a passage, the more important subdivision becomes.

Metric transcriptions involve re-writing the music into another meter, and proportionately scaling all of the rhythms and tempo so that the transcription sounds the same, but may be notated more simply. When transcribing from **simple** to **compound** meters, **triplets** and **sextuplets** become a natural division and subdivision of the beat and are often easier to notate. As long as the tempo of the **beat note** value remains the same, metric transcriptions can be a powerful tool for musicians learning complex rhythms or for creating arrangements for younger performers.

A **rhythmic reduction** notates only the rhythm of a passage and often reveals **rhythmic motives** that make compositions more unified. Rhythmic notation uses slanted, slashes or sometime other shapes instead of normal **noteheads** to specify rhythm without a specific pitch.

Chapter 4 Exercises

1 Division and Subdivision

On the line above each example, provide a complete written division or subdivision of all beats at the level of the smallest note value in that passage, add syllables under those, then add syllables under the lower line (similar to Example 4.5 in the text):

a) (1 beat anacrusis)

b)

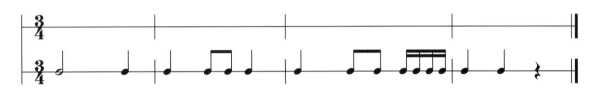

c)

2 Assigning Syllables

Write the correct syllables under each note, then practice reading each out loud:

a) Simple Meters

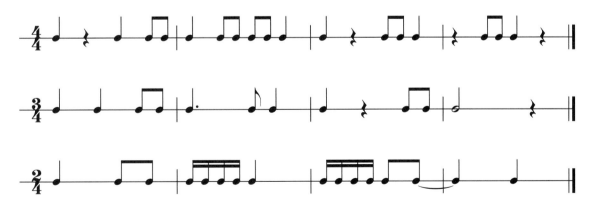

b) Compound Meters

3　Metric Transcription

Transcribe the following into the requested meter so that they sound the same:

a)

b)

c)

4　Rhythmic Reduction

Provide a Rhythmic Reduction for this excerpt and bracket any reoccurring motives you find:

Bach: Suite No. 1 for Solo Cello, Mvt. 3

5 Beginning Rhythmic Reading Exercises

Practice reading these exercises out loud while conducting the patterns shown in Example 3.3. Do not write the syllables underneath, but rather, read them from the notation. Don't forget to mentally divide or subdivide the beats as needed.

a) Simple Meter

i)

ii)

iii)

iv)

b) Compound Meter

(the number of beats to conduct is given before each example):

i) (2)

ii) (3)

iii) (2)

iv) (2)

CHAPTER 5

Pitch and the Musical Keyboard

5.1 Pitch Classes and the Musical Keyboard

Pitch is one of the basic building blocks of music. To talk about pitch in general, English-speaking cultures use a series of seven letters, **A**, **B**, **C**, **D**, **E**, **F**, and **G** to refer to pitch. These letters are called the **pitch names** or sometimes simply **letter names**. These pitch names correspond to the **white key** pattern found on musical keyboards and pianos, as shown in Example 5.1. The **black keys** occur between some white keys in a repeating pattern of groups of two and three, and will be discussed shortly. This pattern repeats over and over across the length of the musical keyboard. You can locate the key that corresponds to C by remembering that it is always the white key directly to the left of the group of two black keys. Although A is the first letter of our alphabet, the pitch C holds a special place in common practice music, as this and future chapters will describe.

 Example 5.1
The musical keyboard—white keys

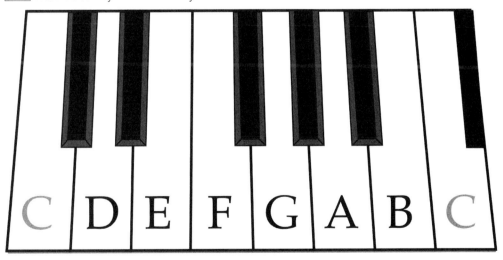

Notice how the first and last notes in Example 5.1 sounded similar. Although both are labeled with the name C, most people would say that the second one sounds "higher" than the first. This is because of the relationship between the **frequencies**: the lower one has a frequency of 261.6 Hz, and the higher one does have a higher frequency—exactly twice the frequency of the lower one (523.2 Hz). This relationship is called an **octave**, from the prefix "octa" meaning eight (notice that there are eight white keys in an octave, including both Cs.) When two pitches have the same letter name, they belong to the same **pitch class**. Each of the seven letters used for general reference to pitches is called a **pitch class**, and generically refers to that note in any octave. Since general, **tonal** relationships between notes are the same (equivalent) regardless of the octave in which they occur, many topics in music theory will only refer to the pitch class as a means of simplification. The term for this relationship between all pitches in a pitch class (i.e. all of the Cs on the keyboard) is **octave equivalence**, and knowing this essential principle is crucial for understanding and analyzing music.

In addition to the white keys, the narrow, black keys were added to fill in the unequal acoustic spaces between notes within each octave. As you listen to Example 5.1 again, notice that the space between C and D is larger than the space between E and F. Now, listen to Example 5.2 and notice how the space between each pitch is perfectly even. These twelve pitches form an equally spaced division of the **octave**, and the space between each adjacent key is called a **half step**. A **whole step** consists of two half steps. As you listen to Example 5.1 again, notice that there is the space of a whole step between all of the white keys on the keyboard except for between E and F, and between B and C. Between these two sets there is only a half step.

Example 5.2
The musical keyboard—black keys

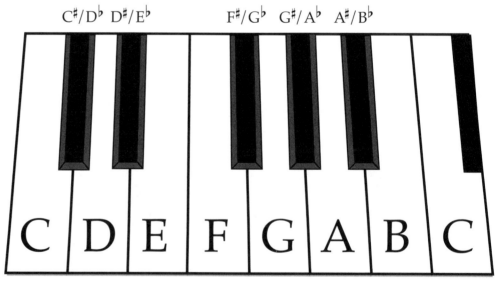

The black keys on the keyboard derive their pitch class name from the white keys nearest them, called the "natural" keys. Each can be identified by a pitch class **letter name** and one of the following symbols, called an **accidental**: a **natural** (♮) refers to the unaltered pitch class letter (white key); a **sharp** (♯) raises the pitch one half step; a **flat** (♭) lowers the pitch one half step. When reading letter names with accidentals, the letter is read first and the accidental is placed after it, as in "A♯" read as "A-sharp."

Using this system, the pitch a **half step** above C (the black key to the right of C) is called C-sharp. That same key on the musical keyboard can also be thought of as a half step below D, or **D-flat**. Each of the black keys has two possible names, as shown above. This relationship between pitches that "overlap" and occur on the same piano key is called an **enharmonic** relationship. F-sharp is **enharmonically equivalent** to G-flat. Notice that they are *equivalent* not the *same*. Although they may sound the same on the musical keyboard, they are actually two distinct pitches that function differently in tonal music, and performers on non-keyboard instruments may adjust the frequency slightly differently between each. Since this difference is very small, and retuning a piano during a performance is impossible, keyboard manufacturers have settled on a tuning system called **equal temperament** (equal tuning) that compromises this slight difference to an acceptable level.

There are two types of half steps, and both are enharmonically equivalent: a **diatonic half step** is one in which each of the two notes has a different letter name (e.g. G-sharp up to A) while a **chromatic half step** is a half step where both notes use the same letter name but different **accidentals** (e.g. A-flat up to A-natural). When a pitch is changed into its enharmonic equivalent, it is said to have been **enharmonically respelled**. These terms will become particularly important in future chapters.

Sometimes it is desirable to raise or lower a pitch by two half steps, and there are **accidentals** for this as well. A **double flat** (♭♭) means the pitch is lowered one **whole step**. A **double sharp** (×) means the pitch is raised one whole step.

Notice that the use of double sharps and double flats will often result in a pitch on the keyboard that can be enharmonically specified without an accidental. For example, G-double-flat is enharmonically equivalent to F-natural; B-double-sharp is enharmonically equivalent to both C-sharp and D-flat. Although it is tempting to use the enharmonically equivalent note name, this would change the function and sometimes even make the notation of the surrounding music more confusing. In most cases, composers and publishers have particular reasons for specifying a certain spelling of a note.

5.2 Specific Pitch and the Modern Keyboard

A standard, modern piano keyboard has a pattern of the above 12 black and white keys repeated seven times (plus four extra keys) for a total of 88 keys (earlier keyboards had fewer keys, as do some electronic and other non-piano keyboards and some modern keyboards add additional keys to extend the lower limit). As you progress "up" the keyboard from left to right, each C is a pitch two times the **frequency** of the C directly below it. Since all **octaves** exist in this relationship, one often speaks of pitch in general terms, such as "The band is playing the pitches C, E-flat, and G." However, when specifying a **specific pitch** in a particular octave, there are two ways musicians have commonly done this.

Example 5.3
The modern 88-key piano keyboard and octave systems

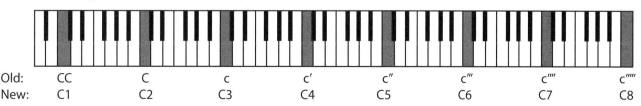

Old:	CC	C	c	c′	c″	c‴	c⁗	c′′′′′
New:	C1	C2	C3	C4	C5	C6	C7	C8

In the old system the lowest C (C1 in the new system) was called "Contra C" (CC), the next was referred to as "Great C" (C2), then "small C" (C3), and each successive octave received a superscript mark and is commonly read in English as "C one," "C two," etc.

The new system is more commonly used today and is used exclusively when referring to electronic musical keyboards. This new system is the one that will be used in this text.

In both systems, the octave designation is determined by the lowest C in that octave. All of the pitches above each C carry the same octave designation until the next C. This means that the note to the right of C4 is called D4, the white key to the right of that is E4, and so forth until reaching the next C, which would be C5. Using this system, the lowest note commonly on the piano is A0, and the highest is C8.

Since the new system has only come into existence recently, many common orchestral instruments use the old system (which was the only one in existence when they were created) when describing the pitch on which they are constructed: a BB♭ tuba, for example, is constructed with contra B-flat (B♭ 1) as its acoustic basis. Most of the lower musical instruments that have their lowest note in this lowest octave carry the prefix "contra" in their name (i.e. contrabass bassoon, contrabass clarinet, etc.).

C4 (or c′ in the old system) is often referred to as "**Middle C**" not only because it occurs roughly in the middle of the piano, but also because it occupies a central location in our musical **notation** system, as shown in the next section.

5.3 Musical Notation using Staves and Clefs

While letters are fine when speaking about music in general, they are not very practical when actually reading or playing music. In Western, common practice **musical notation**, pitch is notated with slanted ovals called **noteheads** on a system of five **lines** and four **spaces** called a **staff** (plural: **staves**). Each line and space specifies a specific pitch in ascending order from bottom to top and is numbered from bottom to top. In this way, one can refer to any line or space by its number.

Example 5.4
The five-line musical staff

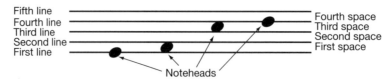

At the beginning of the staff there is a symbol called a **clef** which tells us what specific pitches are assigned to each of the lines and spaces. To write a pitch that is above or below the five lines of the staff, temporary extensions called **ledger lines** are used to extend the staff and accommodate the new pitches. They are added with the same space between each ledger line as is used in the staff, as shown in Example 5.5.

Example 5.5
The treble clef

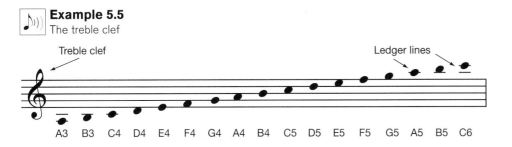

The clef in Example 5.5 is called a **treble clef**. The treble clef is sometimes called a "G-Clef" since it circles the second line, which is G4. C4 (middle C) is located on the first ledger line below the staff. Each line or space indicates a successive pitch.

The next clef commonly used today is the **bass clef**.

Example 5.6
The bass clef

The **bass clef** is used along with the treble clef for the vast majority of music today.

This clef is sometimes referred to as the "F clef" since it circles F3 on the fourth line and further highlights this pitch with its two dots.

Keyboard music uses two staves, one treble clef and one bass clef, which are grouped together into a special set called a **grand staff**. A **brace** is a special curved line on the left that indicates their grouping as a single entity. Each **staff** or group of staves on a page is referred to as a **staff system**. Notice that the note right in the middle is "Middle C"—which is how it got that pitch got its name. This combination of treble and bass clef staves allows for the notation of the most common octaves of pitches used in music, especially those within the vocal range.

Example 5.7
The grand staff and middle C

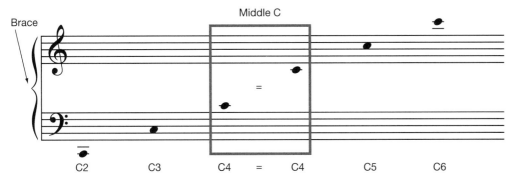

Table 5.1 Ottava Signs

Symbol	Name	How it alters pitch	Written	Actual pitches
8ᵛᵃ	ottava	Sounds one octave above notated pitches		
15ᵐᵃ	quindicesima	Sounds two octaves above notated pitches		
8ᵛᵇ	ottava bassa	Sounds one octave below notated pitches		
15ᵐᵇ	quindicesimabassa	Sounds two octaves below notated pitches		

Even within the grand staff, **ledger lines** are frequently used to extend both above and below each staff. However, when more than three ledger lines are needed for an extended period of time, composers and publishers will often use an **ottava** (Italian for "octave") symbol to indicate that the pitches are notated in a different **octave** to avoid the need for numerous ledger lines (and the difficulty in reading them). These are derived from the Italian terms and function as specified in Table 5.1.

Both **alto** and **tenor** clefs use the same symbol for the clef (called a **C clef**), but differ only in the location of the C clef on the **staff**. In both, the center of the C clef "points" to the pitch **Middle C** (C4.) In early music, these C clefs were used extensively for vocal music; however, today, only a few instruments use these two clefs (violas primarily use alto clef, and 'cellos, trombones, and bassoons occasionally use tenor clef).

Example 5.8a
The alto clef

Example 5.8b
The tenor clef

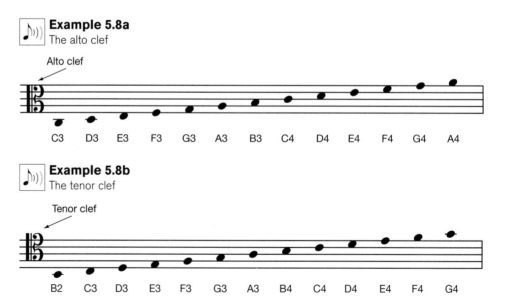

In modern choral and vocal music, tenor parts are notated in a **octave clef** (Example 5.9). This looks just like a **treble clef** with a small "8" at the bottom, which indicates that all of the pitches are one **octave** lower than they would be in a normal treble clef.

Example 5.9
The octave clef for modern vocal tenor parts

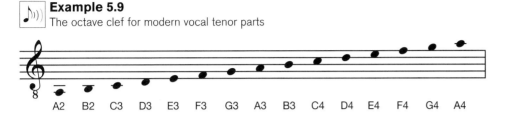

A2 B2 C3 D3 E3 F3 G3 A3 B3 C4 D4 E4 F4 G4 A4

In some cases, rather than making use of **ledger lines** or **ottava** signs, a **clef** change may occur. These may occur at any place in music where they are needed. When they occur at the beginning of a staff system, the clef is full-sized, but when occurring mid-**measure**, they are usually reduced in size, as shown in Example 5.10.

Example 5.10
Changing clef in the middle of a passage

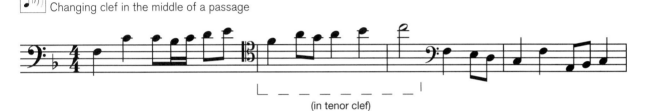

(in tenor clef)

5.4 Whole and Half Steps on the Musical Staff

As all of the previous examples show, the arrangement or **pitch classes** on the **staff** will vary depending on the **clef** that is used. Because there are **whole steps** between some pitch classes (C–D, D–E, F–G, and G–A) but only **half steps** between others (E–F and B–C) the space between each line and space cannot be assumed to be a whole step without regard for which clef is in use. Because many musicians are visual thinkers, and the staff system is a visual, graphic notation system, it may be tempting to think of all lines and spaces being equal in **interval** size, but in fact, depending on the **clef**, they are not.

Example 5.11
Changing arrangements of whole and half steps on the treble and bass clef staves

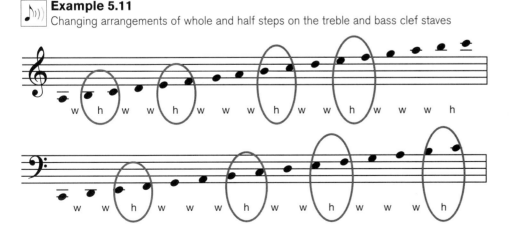

Once a musician makes the shift from visually "calculating" pitches to fluently reading specific pitches, this irregularity of size between some lines and spaces becomes a non-issue. The space between B and C is always a half step, as is E to F, regardless of where it occurs. Therefore, in order to study music, one needs to be able to do more than just know the right fingering on one's instrument for a given note on a staff: one must also know the **specific pitch** for that note. This makes reading musical pitches in all standard clefs one of the most basic and standard skills for all aspiring musicians.

5.5 Notating Accidentals

When notating **accidentals**, they always are placed directly *before* the **notehead**, centered on the same line or space as the notehead, but still read aloud *after* the letter name. An accidental remains in effect until the end of a measure unless canceled by use of a **natural** or other accidental. Although not required, when a passage of music contains many accidentals, **cautionary accidentals** (also known as **courtesy accidentals**) are added in parenthesis as helpful reminders that the accidental in the previous measure is no longer applied.

Example 5.12
Use of accidentals in musical notation

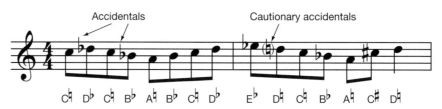

5.6 Reading Music Pitches

Most instrumentalists learn to read pitches only on the staff that their instrument uses, and some vocalists learn to sing by ear (oral tradition). All musicians, however, should be able to read music in all clefs fluently in order to communicate with other musicians and understand the wide range of musical examples that any advanced music studies will entail. Although there are many memory aids on the Internet and in some textbooks that can help you figure out pitches in unfamiliar clefs (such as memorizing a non-musical saying such as "Every Good Boy Does Fine" to recall the lines of the **treble clef staff**), these only allow a student to calculate pitch. Each aspiring musician should make it a personal goal to move beyond these aids and to be able to easily and fluently *read* music. The following tips should help in mastering note reading:

1. *Focus on learning the **natural** notes first.*
   All sharp and flat notes have the same letter name as the naturals, so focus on learning only the natural **letter names** first, then add whatever accidental is on the **notehead**.

2. *Don't try to learn too much at a time.*
   Focus on only one **clef** at a time (beginning with treble and bass clefs first, since they are the most common) and practice memorizing only a few **natural** notes (five or six) at a time. Begin with the "easy" pitches around **Middle C** for C clefs, and in familiar areas of the other clefs, then work your way out from there in subsequent days.

Using this method, most students can memorize half of a staff worth of note names per day. With only four common clefs (treble, alto, tenor, and bass) this requires only eight days worth of work to master all four! Considering most musicians already read one clef fluently, this makes the task even simpler.

3. *Read the pitches out loud.*
   Reading the pitch names out loud uses a different part of the brain than just "thinking about them" and will cause the mind to remember them faster and longer. Set your **metronome** to 60–90 beats per minute and try to read the end of chapter drills at that speed until there is no hesitation.

4. *Practice, practice, practice—with patience!*
   No new language is learned in a day or by simple tricks or phrases. Many aspiring musicians feel frustrated when learning a new clef does not come quickly, but it helps to remember that when first beginning musical studies, it probably took weeks or even months to learn the basic notes of one's primary clef. If two or three days of dedicated memorization and drill is devoted to each clef (and every new skill in this text), this is, by comparison, a very small amount of time and should be viewed as a sign of your ever increasing musical abilities, not a frustration.

The **supplemental, interactive drills** have been designed to help you to learn to read fluently in all common clefs, and all that is required is patient, focused, and dedicated practice to master the basic symbols of our musical language. There may be some, however, that learn differently, and your teacher and other musicians may have tips and techniques like the memory aids discussed above that can help you to learn these valuable skills. However, if any memory aid is used, it should be used only as a crutch until you are able to fluently read all **clefs** without hesitation.

Chapter Summary

The **musical keyboard** consists of a repeating pattern containing seven **white keys** and five **black keys** that play the 12 **pitch classes** of the Western musical system. Each repetition plays the 12 pitch classes in a different **octave**. **Specific pitch** indicates both the pitch class and the octave in which it exists. The white keys play **natural** notes, which in the English-speaking countries are generally referred to by **letter names** A, B, C, D, E, F, and G. **Middle C** is a specific pitch that occupies a central place both on the musical keyboard and in our common practice notational system. There are two systems of identifying specific pitch: the older, historical system with c′ as Middle C, and the new, modern system, which numbers octaves with C4 as Middle C, and is the system used in this text.

The acoustic distance between each key, whether black or white, is a **half step**. A **diatonic half step** is one in which each of the two notes has a different **letter name**, while a **chromatic half step** is a half step where both notes have as their root the same letter name but use different **accidentals**. There are black keys between each white key except between E and F, and B and C, which have white keys only a half step apart. An **accidental** is a symbol placed before a **notehead** or after a letter name to alter the pitch. A **flat** lowers a note by one half step, while a **sharp** raises it by a half step. A **double sharp** raises a pitch by two half steps and a **double flat** lowers it by that same amount. Accidentals remain in effect throughout a **measure** of music. A **cautionary accidental** is placed in parenthesis and used as an optional reminder that the accidental in the previous measure is no longer in effect. **Enharmonically equivalent** notes are those which have two spellings that both occupy the same key on the keyboard.

Pitch is notated in common practice notation on a **staff** consisting of five **lines** separated by four equally sized spaces. Each natural pitch class occupies a line or a space. **Ledger lines** extend above or below the staff to allow higher or lower pitches to be notated. A **clef** at the beginning of each staff defines which specific pitch is assigned to each line and space. The four commonly encountered modern staves are **treble**, **alto**, **tenor**, and **bass**. A **grand staff** consists of a treble and bass clef connected together as a set and linked with a **brace**. Middle C is the pitch occupying the first ledger line above the bass clef and the first ledger line below the treble clef, in the middle of the grand staff. Pitches occurring in extreme registers may be notated in a more simple to read octave by use of an **ottava** sign or a temporary change of clef.

Note Reading Drill

Read the following pitches out loud, applying the treble, bass, alto, and tenor clefs. Begin with the clef most familiar to you, and progress to the less familiar ones. Focus on only one measure at a time until it is mastered before moving on to the next. Continue this exercise until you can read it at one note per second with zero mistakes or hesitations in all clefs (this may take several class periods). The class may try this or a similar exercise as a game of "elimination" for fun. Who can read it the fastest?

Example 5.13

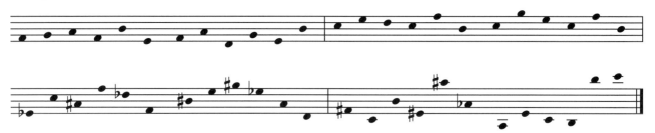

Chapter 5 Exercises

1   Whole and Half Steps
Provide the requested pitch class name:

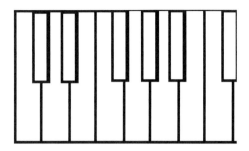

a) diatonic half step above G: _____

b) diatonic whole step above E: _____

c) whole step below C: _____

d) chromatic half step below A♭:   _____

e) chromatic half step above E: _____

f) chromatic half step below C: _____

2   Enharmonic Equivalence
Fill in the blanks.

a) What pitch class is enharmonically equivalent to G♯?_____

b) What are the enharmonic spellings of the pitch class two whole steps above
     A? _____ and _____

c) Name two pitch classes that are enharmonically equivalent to G natural:
     _____ and _____.

3 Draw a line from the pitches to the correct note on the keyboard, then fill in that
     key with your pencil (C4 has been done for you as an example):

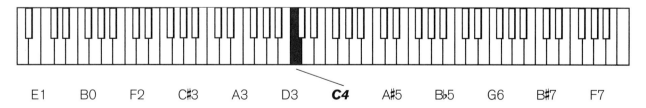

E1   B0   F2   C♯3   A3   D3   *C4*   A♯5   B♭5   G6   B♯7   F7

4   Identify the requested specific pitches on the keyboard, including enharmonic equivalents if requested:

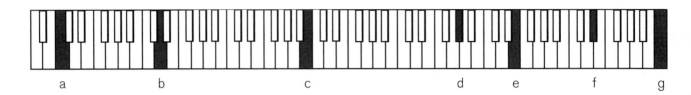

a) _____

b) _____

c) _____ or _____

d) _____ or _____

e) _____ or _____

f) _____ or _____

g) _____ or _____

5   First, read the following pitches out loud (as letter names only) several times, then write the specific pitch (including octave) under each notehead:

6   Renotate the following examples using the given ottava sign:

a)

b)

(all in bass clef)

7   Add cautionary accidentals where needed:

CHAPTER 6

Chromatic, Modal, and Major Scales

6.1 The Chromatic Scale

A **scale** is an ordered pattern of **pitch classes** that fill in the space of an **octave** and repeat in the same pattern in all octaves. This pattern may be composed of any number of pitch classes in any pattern. One of the most basic scales is the **chromatic scale**, which consists of all 12 pitch classes. The distance between each of the 12 pitch classes in the chromatic scale is called a **half step** or semitone.

Example 6.1
The chromatic scale, ascending using sharps, descending using flats

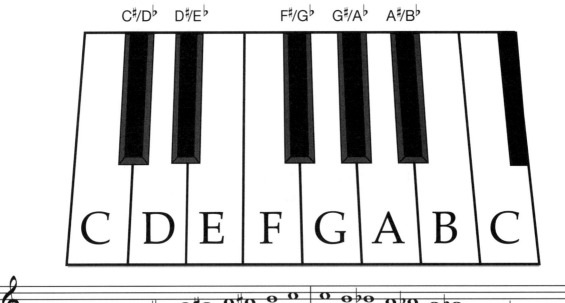

Notice that the chromatic scale may be spelled using only **sharps** or only **flats**, and that it may be spelled using **diatonic half steps** or **chromatic half steps**, but it sounds the same when played on a keyboard (this is the **enharmonic relationship** discussed in the **previous chapter**). Although the chromatic scale may be correctly spelled using any combination of sharps or flats, composers usually will use sharps when the chromatic scale is ascending, and flats when it is descending, or whichever means uses the fewest **accidentals**. When spelling the various types of **tonal** and **modal** scales that do not use all 12 pitch classes, it does become very important which spelling is used.

6.2 Historical Background: The Modes

The music of the common practice period is based on seven-note scales that use a different **letter name** for each note of the scale and use each letter name only once. The term for this is **diatonic**. As noted in the **previous chapter,** "**Pitch and the Musical Keyboard,**" the white keys do not have a consistent space between each key as does the chromatic scale. Prior to this period, as tonal music was in its early stage of development, composers wrote music that did not make use of all 12 chromatic notes. A specific pattern of half steps (h) and whole steps (w) emerged which today is represented by the **white key notes** on the musical keyboard and the lines and spaces on our musical **staff**. Each scale based on a (white key) natural pitch class will have a different pattern of whole and half steps, resulting in a different sound or feel. These scales are referred to as **modes**. Table 6.1 lists all of the modes constructed from only the natural pitch classes (A, B, C, D, E, F, and G). Note that each modal scale begins on a different letter name. When identifying modes, one also includes the letter name upon which they begin, as in "Aeolian on A", "Locrian on B", etc. Listen to each one several times and notice how the changing patterns of whole and half steps create a different sound for each mode.

Table 6.1 The modes

Mode	Starting pitch	Notated as	Audio example
Aeolian	A	w h w w h w w	🎵
Locrian	B	h w w h w w w	🎵
Ionian (major scale)	C	w w h w w w h	🎵
Dorian	D	w h w w w h w	🎵
Phrygian	E	h w w w h w w	🎵
Lydian	F	w w w h w w h	🎵
Mixolydian	G	w h w w h w w	🎵

The names for these modes come from ancient Greeks who used them to link their musical sound to different emotions (even though the names are historically documented, no audio examples of actual Greek modes exist, so today no one knows the exact pitch-patterns to which each mode refers). Theorists of the fourteenth century adopted these Greek names to study and name their modes. After this period, some of these modes were preferred over others. As the **common practice period** developed, two modes, the **Ionian** and **Aeolian**, were used most often. It is important to note, however, that many composers of the twentieth and twenty-first centuries and jazz performers today use the other modes in their music. The Ionian mode is better known today as the **major scale** and the Aeolian as the **natural minor scale**.

Early instruments were constructed to play primarily these seven-note scales and only later added mechanisms that could play in-between the whole steps. This is why flutes, clarinets, and most woodwinds have "side keys" and why the chromatic **black keys** on the musical keyboard are smaller. This is also why our modern five-line staves have half steps between the notes E and F and between B and C but whole steps between all other pitch classes.

6.3 The Major Scale

 Example 6.2
The major scale starting on C

As previously noted (see Table 6.1), the Ionian scale pattern forms the **major scale**. It is a succession of two whole steps, a half step, three whole steps, and finally one half step, which returns it to the same **pitch class** upon which it began. It is this pattern of whole and half steps that gives the major scale its characteristic sound.

Scale degree numbers are used to refer generically to the notes in common seven-note scales. Scale degree numbers always have the small **caret** symbol (^) above them and are read as: "scale degree one," etc. The C major scale pattern labeled via scale degree numbers would look like this:

Example 6.3
The major scale pattern

C D E F C A B C
1̂ 2̂ 3̂ 4̂ 5̂ 6̂ 7̂ 1̂
w w h w w w h

Obviously, not all music is in C major. In fact, one important trait of common practice music rests on the concept that any of the 12 pitch classes can serve as scale degree 1. All major scales beginning on any pitch must have the exact same pattern of whole and half steps (*wwhwwwh*). **Transposition** is the process of taking any pattern and moving the whole thing so that it is replicated exactly beginning on another pitch. Any major scale can be created by transposing the pattern of *wwhwwwh* to begin on any pitch. However, when a scale begins on a pitch other than C, each **scale degree** still must be on a separate line or space and have a different **letter name**. But, because of the unequal nature of the musical staff system, each major scale except C will need to have one or more notes altered with an **accidental** to form the major scale pattern of whole and half steps. For example, if you start the major scale pattern on a G, you will need to add a **sharp** to the F to raise it a half step in order to form a whole step between scale degrees 6 and 7.

Example 6.4
The G major scale

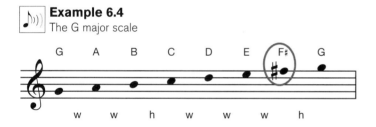

You would not spell this note G-flat, since that would result in a scale with no "F" and two "G"s and every major or minor scale must have a different letter name for each scale degree with no duplicates.

Notice how easy it is to discuss any major scale using scale degrees: in any **major scale**, scale degree 3 will always be a half step below scale degree 4; and there is always a half step between scale degree 7 and scale degree 1 above it. All other scale degrees will have whole steps between them in any major key. Although the starting note may change, the relationship between each scale degree remains consistent in all major scales. This is a powerful tool in helping musicians to memorize their major scales and to talk about music in general.

Take for example, the major scales beginning on C-sharp and D-flat. If the pattern of *wwhwwwh* is applied to each, the following scales will result (Example 6.5):

Example 6.5

C-sharp and D-flat major scales

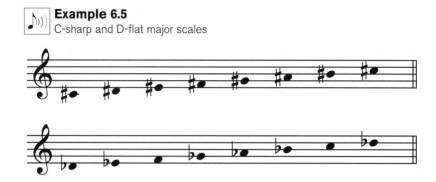

In both scales, every scale degree is an **enharmonic equivalent** of the same scale degree in the other. The scale degree 5 in C-sharp major, G-sharp, is the enharmonic equivalent of A-flat, which is also scale degree 5 in D-flat major. In fact, since all of the scale degrees are enharmonically equivalent, it can be said that C-sharp major and D-flat major are **enharmonically equivalent scales**. The same can be said of F-sharp and G-flat, and C-flat and B-natural major scales. In each of these cases, either major scale can be enharmonically respelled into the other with no omissions or duplications of letter names, and all scale degrees will function in the same manner. This principle allows composers to choose a key that is easier to read without losing any functionality (for example, choosing B major rather than C-flat major).

6.4 Scale Degree Names

Another way of referring to the members of the major scale is by their function. The functional names of each scale degree are listed in Table 6.2.

Table 6.2 Scale degree names

$\hat{1}$	$\hat{2}$	$\hat{3}$	$\hat{4}$	$\hat{5}$	$\hat{6}$	$\hat{7}$
Tonic	Supertonic	Mediant	Subdominant	Dominant	Submediant	Leading tone

These names are derived from their function in the scale, and knowing these functions can be helpful in memorizing them. **Tonic** is the most important, and is the tone that identifies each scale by name. The **leading tone** "leads" up to tonic. The **dominant** also functions harmonically in a very important (dominant) way, only surpassed by the tonic, hence its name. **Mediant** comes from the term "median" or middle, and is in the middle between the tonic and dominant. As the prefix "sub" (below) would imply, the **subdominant** is the same distance *below* tonic as the dominant is above it. Similarly, the **submediant** is midway between tonic and the subdominant. "Super" (above) refers to the scale degree above tonic: the **supertonic**.

Example 6.6 clearly shows these functional names in their above/below tonic relationship. Notice that for the dominant and subdominant (or any scale degree) the same **pitch class** in any **octave** also goes by the same name as well.

Example 6.6

Scale degree names and relationships

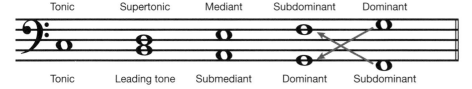

Chapter Summary

A **scale** is an ordered pattern of **pitch classes** that fill in the space of an **octave** and repeats in the same pattern in all octaves. The **chromatic scale** consists of all **half steps** (or **semitones**) and may be spelled with either sharps or flats. A **diatonic** scale uses a different pitch **letter name** for each member of the scale, without any duplicate letters. The seven **modes** are all possible diatonic scales using only the **white keys** on the **keyboard**.

Of these, the **Ionian mode** is now used as our **major scale**. All major scales have seven **scale degrees**, separated by the following pattern of whole (w) and half (h) steps: *wwhwwwh*. **Transposition** allows any pattern to be recreated exactly beginning upon another pitch, and allows for 12 uniquely sounding major scales, each beginning on a different pitch class. **Enharmonically equivalent** scales are those in which all seven **scale degrees** may be enharmonically respelled into another major scale that sounds the same yet may be easier to read. All major scales except C major will require **chromatic alteration** to form the major scale pattern.

Each scale degree has a functional name: **tonic**, **supertonic**, **mediant**, **subdominant**, **dominant**, **submediant**, and the **leading tone**, respectively (ascending).

Rhythmic Reading Exercises

First, try sight reading each of the following rhythms out loud, using the counting system from **Chapter 4**. Then count while conducting. Finally, practice these until mastered at a brisk **tempo**. Remember: always read these out loud every time—thinking the counting is like "thinking about practicing," it isn't really practice! It is best not to write in the rhythm syllables.

Simple Meter

Compound Meter

Chapter 6 Exercises

1 Write a chromatic scale one octave as requested from the given note and provide two enharmonically related spellings for the requested note:

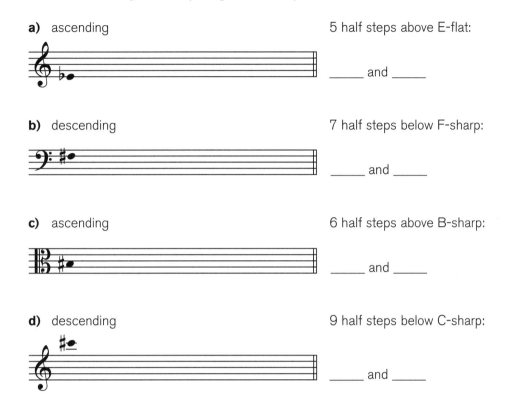

a) ascending   5 half steps above E-flat:

_____ and _____

b) descending   7 half steps below F-sharp:

_____ and _____

c) ascending   6 half steps above B-sharp:

_____ and _____

d) descending   9 half steps below C-sharp:

_____ and _____

2 Write the chromatic scale segment between the given notes. Do not use double flats and double sharps:

a) use only naturals and sharps   **b)** use only naturals and flats

3 Fill in the blanks:

a) What note is 4 half steps below D♯4? _____ or _____

b) What note is 2 whole steps and one diatonic half step above B2? _____

c) C♯6 is 2 chromatic half steps above _____.

d) C3 is 3 diatonic half steps above _____.

e) How many whole steps between E♭3 and A2? _____

f) How many half steps are between F♯3 and D♭4? _____

4 Identify the mode and label the whole (w) and half (h) steps between each scale degree:

a)

Mode: _____

b)

Mode: _____

5 Underneath each collection, write the *wwhwwwh* pattern that characterizes the major scale. Next, add accidentals to the appropriate notes so that the result matches the major scale pattern. Do not change the first or last note:

a)   **b)**

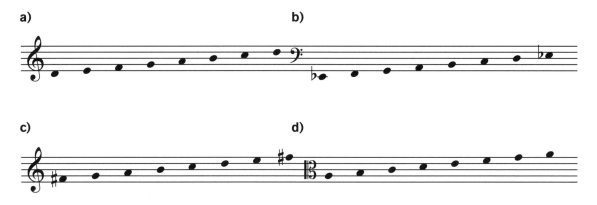

c)   **d)**

6 Circle the notes that are not a part of the specified major scale:

a) D major   **b)** E major   **c)** F major

7 Fill in the blanks:

a) The dominant is scale degree: _____

b) The mediant is scale degree: _____

c) The _____ is 5 scale degrees below tonic.

d) The _____ is 5 scale degrees above the supertonic.

e) The _____ is 4 scale degrees below the mediant.

CHAPTER 7

Tendency Tones and Minor Scales

7.1 Tendency Tones

As defined in the **previous chapter**, the **major scale** has the following pattern of whole and half steps:

Example 7.1
The major scale pattern

This pattern results in two **diatonic half steps**: one between **scale degrees** 3 and 4, and another between scale degrees 7 and 1. As you listen to this example, notice how strongly scale degree 7 "pulls" toward the **tonic** as the scale ascends. When a certain tone has a strong pull toward another, it is called a **tendency tone**. In musical practice, composers tend to fulfill the desire of the leading note to "resolve" up to tonic, hence the name. Notes that are only a half step apart commonly function as tendency tones. Notice that scale degree 4, F, also is only a half step from E and in **tonal** music has a tendency in melodies to often resolve down to scale degree 3, especially when approached from above. However, since scale degree 7 pulls toward the most stable pitch in the scale, the tonic, it is the most important tendency tone.

Example 7.2
Tendency tones in the major scale

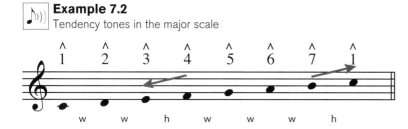

Tendency tones function a lot like magnets: as a pitch gets closer to an important tone, such as tonic or **dominant**, it has a tendency to be heard as wanting to be pulled or resolved toward that tone. This is especially noticeable when listening to the difference between the **whole steps** verses the **half steps** in the scale. These half-step tendency tones play an important part in the function of tonal music, not only in major keys but also in minor keys as well.

Example 7.3
Tendency tones

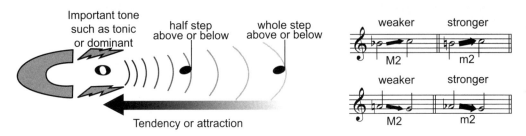

7.2 The Natural Minor Scale

Besides the **Ionian** mode, which in tonal music became the major scale, the **Aeolian** mode was also very popular and became our **natural minor scale**. It is called the natural minor scale because there are no **chromatic** changes from this original, modal "natural" state.

Example 7.4
The natural minor scale

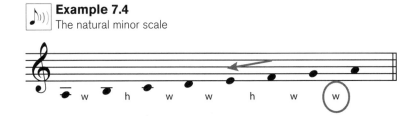

Although the pattern of whole and half steps has changed significantly from the major scale (*whwwhww*) the scale degree names are almost the same as those of the major scale, with one notable exception:

Table 7.1 Natural minor scale degree names

Scale degree number	$\hat{1}$	$\hat{2}$	$\hat{3}$	$\hat{4}$	$\hat{5}$	$\hat{6}$	$\hat{7}$
Scale degree name	Tonic	Supertonic	Mediant	Sub-dominant	Dominant	Sub-mediant	Sub-tonic

You may have noticed, like many early composers, that in natural minor scale degree 7 is a whole step away from scale degree 1, eliminating that desirable **tendency tone** which strengthens the tonic of the scale. Since it is no longer a half step "leading" up to tonic, its function has changed, and it is now called the **subtonic** (below-tonic). Instead, there is now a half step between scale degrees 5 and 6. In minor scales, this creates a strong tendency for the weaker **submediant** to pull down to the more important dominant:

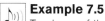

Example 7.5
Tendency of the lowered submediant toward the dominant

Although this new tendency tone has a pleasant and desirable effect, many composers found that when adding **harmonies** to their scales (a process that will be covered in greater detail in later chapters), they needed to raise scale degree 7 by a **chromatic half step** (making it a **leading tone**) to recreate the same upward tendency tone to tonic that occurs in the major scale. This resulted in the creation of the **harmonic minor scale**.

7.3 The Harmonic Minor Scale

Example 7.6
The harmonic minor scale

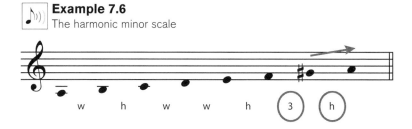

As you listen to this scale, notice how strongly scale degree 7 pulls up to tonic, since it is now functioning as a leading tone, as it did in the major scale. But, notice how there is now a space larger than a whole step between scale degrees 6 and 7 (it has a span of three half-steps!). This gives melodies using this scale an exotic sound.

Example 7.7
Melody using the G harmonic minor scale

Although this space is common in music of the Near and Middle East, in common practice music this is considered awkward and difficult to sing. This led to the use of a third form of the minor scale, which became the most frequently used form of minor scale in common practice melodies.

7.4 The Melodic Minor Scale

Example 7.8
The melodic minor scale

The **melodic minor scale** has two forms: ascending and descending. The ascending form has a pattern of *whwwwwh*, and is created by altering the **natural minor scale** by raising scale degrees 6 and 7 a **chromatic half step**. Notice that this alters the upper four notes of the scale to form the same notes that would be found in the major scale. The descending form uses the natural minor scale form (*whwwhww*, when viewed from bottom to top). With this simple change, this scale keeps the strong tendency tones of both major and natural minor. The ascending form strengthens the tendency toward tonic by eliminating the lowered **submediant** and adding the leading tone, but when lowered to their **natural** state on the descending form, they once again have a tendency to pull down to the dominant. In fact, from the dominant up to tonic, the ascending form of the melodic minor scale is identical to the major scale (*wwwh*). Notice that this form also avoids the awkward "larger than a whole step" space that was formed in the **harmonic minor scale**. The following melody uses the melodic form of the minor scale. Notice how when resolving up to tonic, scale degree 6 and 7 are raised, but when leading downward to the dominant they are lowered, and that whenever they are next to one another both are always altered in the same way.

Example 7.9
Melody using the E melodic minor scale: Bach, Suite in E minor for Lute, BWV 996, V, "Bourée"

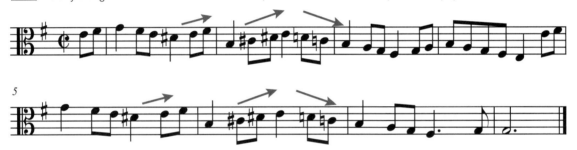

Whenever notating a **melodic minor scale**, you must always include both ascending and descending forms. Although the name for scale degree 6 always remains the submediant, when raised, scale degree 7 must be referred to as the **leading tone**, and when lowered as the **subtonic**.

7.5 Spelling Minor Scales

Like major scales, all minor scales may be **transposed** to begin on any **pitch class**, as long as the scale pattern is the same. When spelling minor scales, the same rules apply as for major scales: each scale degree must have a separate and unique **letter name**, and use **accidentals** to alter these letter names to form the correct pattern of half, whole, or in the case of harmonic minor, the three-half-step space between scale degrees 6 and 7.

Many beginning musicians try to spell all minor scales beginning with the major scale, then using **accidentals** to alter it into the natural minor scale, and then altering it again into the harmonic or melodic forms of minor scale. As this description demonstrates, this is a rather complicated method of spelling a scale. A more simple and direct method is to begin with the natural minor scale pattern of *whwwhww*. For the first five scale degrees, all three forms of the minor scale are the same. Then, it is a simple task to raise scale degree 7 to form the harmonic minor scale, or to raise both scale degrees 6 and 7 on the ascending form of the melodic minor scale. It is even easier if this is done as the **notehead** is being written on the page. Although it may seem a bit slow at first, with a little practice this process will become quite simple. An added benefit is that the process is the same whether one is writing scales using letter names, notating noteheads on a staff, or playing them on one's instrument: the pattern of spaces between scale degrees leads from one note to the next in the same manner in all three cases. As students learn to write scales, it is important to also learn to play them on their instruments and to sing them. By integrating all these means of expressing a scale, the process becomes more and more simple and applicable to making music.

Example 7.10
Spelling minor scales

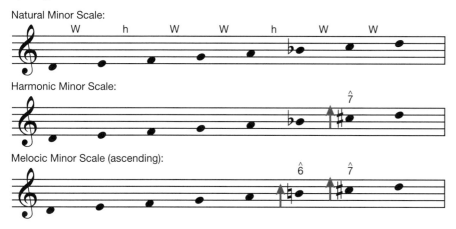

Notice that for minor scales beginning on G-sharp, D-sharp, and A-sharp, this will require the use of **double sharps** to form the harmonic and melodic forms of these minor scales. Although uncommon, there are compositions written in these keys. Like major scales, these three keys may be **enharmonically** respelled into A-flat, E-flat, and B-flat minor, respectively, which greatly simplifies their spelling, as shown in Example 7.11. For this reason the simpler, flat spellings are more commonly encountered.

Example 7.11
Enharmonically equivalent minor scales

Chapter Summary

There is a musical "pull," or desire to resolve to a more stable tone of the scale, exerted between notes separated by **half steps** in a scale, and these are called **tendency tones**. In major scales, scale degree 7 tends to resolve up to **tonic**, and when approached from above, scale degree 4 tends to resolve down to scale degree 3. The strongest tendency tone is the **leading tone**, which moves up a half step toward tonic.

The **natural minor scale** pattern is based on the **Aeolian** modal scale, and has the pattern of: *whwwhww*. This scale contains a seventh scale degree which is a **whole step** below tonic, and this is called the **subtonic**. The subtonic has a lesser tendency to resolve up to tonic than the leading tone. Since scale degree 6 is only a half step above the more stable dominant (scale degree 5) in the natural minor scale, it has a tendency to resolve down to the **dominant**.

The **harmonic minor scale** has a pattern of *whwwh3h*, and uses a raised seventh scale degree which converts the **subtonic** back into a **leading tone**. Although this emphasizes the tonic once again, it does create an awkward interval of three half steps between scale degrees 6 and 7, giving it an exotic feel that is not frequently used in **common practice** music.

The **melodic minor scale** is used frequently in common practice music. It uses the natural minor scale (*whwwhww*) for descending passages, but in order to retain the leading tone and avoid the three-half-step interval found in the harmonic minor scale, it raises both scale degrees 6 and 7 in ascending passages in order to create a smoother melodic line with a pattern of *whwwwwh*.

When spelling minor scales, begin on tonic, then, using a different letter name (or line/space on the staff) for each scale degree, add **accidentals** to form the correct pattern. For the first five notes, the pattern is the same: *whww*. Then begin spelling the remaining scale degrees using the natural minor scale pattern of *hww*, but raise scale degree 6 for the melodic ascending scale, and scale degree 7 for both the harmonic and melodic ascending scale forms. Although the minor scales beginning on G-sharp, D-sharp, and A-sharp are found in music, their more simple, **enharmonic** equivalents A-flat, E-flat, and B-flat minor are more commonly found.

Rhythmic Reading Exercises

Conduct and count these rhythms. Be sure to continue dividing the beat silently during the rests.

Simple Meter

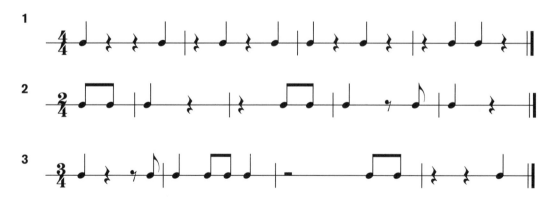

Compound Meter

Constant Tempo Drill

As a class, with eyes closed clap the following exercise, repeating it several times as directed by your instructor. Be sure to remain *totally* silent during the rests (no foot tapping or other sounds) and see how accurately everyone can enter after the rests. Once mastered at two measures rest, double it to four measures rest. Can the class accurately make it through eight measures rest at a constant tempo?

Chapter 7 Exercises

1   Fill in the blanks:

a) In major keys, the tendency tones are scale degrees _____ and _____.

b) In natural minor keys, scale degree 6 tends to pull to scale degree _____.

c) In harmonic minor keys, scale degree 7 tends to pull to scale degree _____.

d) In ascending melodic minor, scale degrees _____ and _____ are raised a half step from the natural minor.

e) The subtonic is a member of what minor scale form(s)?

_____

f) What pitch is the leading tone in g minor? _____

g) What pitch is the leading tone in f minor? _____

h) The only form of the minor scale with a 3 half-step space is the _____ minor scale, and that space is between scale degrees _____ and _____.

2   Fill in the blank to identify the tonic pitch, then underneath each collection, write the *whwwhww* pattern that characterizes the minor scale. Finally, add accidentals to the appropriate notes so that the result matches the natural minor scale pattern. Do not change the first or last notes:

a) ____ natural minor   **b)** ____ natural minor

c) ____ natural minor   **d)** ____ natural minor

3   All minor scale forms use the same pattern for the first five notes (*whww*). Write the first five notes of a minor scale starting with the given note:

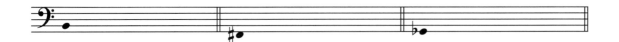

4   Add accidentals to form the minor scales as requested without changing the first or last notes:

natural   harmonic   melodic (ascending)

a)   a minor

b)   d minor

c)   c minor

d)   e minor

5   Write the requested one-octave scales using accidentals:

a)   c harmonic minor   **b)**   e-flat natural minor

c)   f-natural minor   **d)**   e harmonic minor

e)   a-flat harmonic minor   **f)**   d harmonic minor

g)   A-flat major   **h)**   B major

i)   g melodic minor, ascending and descending

j)   d-sharp melodic minor, ascending and descending

Key Signatures

8.1 Key Signatures for Major Keys

A **key signature** displays the **accidentals** that need to be added to any of the seven **scale degrees** in order to form any given **scale**. Any accidental in the key signature effects all **octaves** of that **pitch class**, so a D-flat changes all Ds into D-flats at the same time. In **tonal** music, this is far more efficient than adding a sharp or flat in front of every note, as Example 8.1 demonstrates. Composers expect that musicians will know all scales by memory so that the key signature may serve as only a reminder of the **chromatically** altered pitches. This is why it is essential for musicians to memorize and fluidly master their key signatures and scales for all major and minor **keys**.

 Example 8.1
Schubert, Moment Musical No. 6, mm. 108–115

8.2 Sharp Keys and the Order of Sharps

Arranging all of the major keys that use sharps in their scales, beginning with zero sharps and proceeding up to all seven sharps produces the list of **sharp major key signatures** shown in Example 8.2.

Example 8.2
The sharp major key signatures

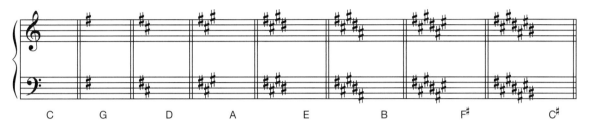

The location of each sharp on the staff is very important and specific. An F-sharp always goes on the top line of the treble clef, and the second from the top line of the bass clef. Although some early music (pre-**common practice**) may not conform exactly to the above pattern, music from the common practice period forward does.

Hint for recognizing sharp major key signatures: When learning to recognize major key signatures in sharp keys, a simple method is to remember that the last sharp in the key signature is always the **leading tone**, which is one scale degree (a **diatonic half step**) below the **tonic**, which is the name of the **key**. For example, the last sharp in the major key with three sharps is G-sharp and a half-step above this is A. And indeed, three sharps is the key signature for A major. Example 8.3 illustrates this process for all sharp keys (remember to include the sharps in the key signature when determining the tonic for F-sharp and C-sharp!).

Example 8.3
Recognizing sharp major key signatures

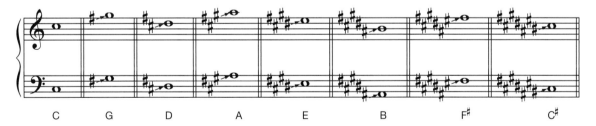

8.3 Flat Key Signatures and the Order of Flats

Just as the sharp keys have a certain order in which the sharps are arranged in a key signature, so too do flat keys. Arranging all of the major keys that use flats in their scales, beginning with zero flats and proceeding up to all seven flats, results in the list of **flat major key signatures** found in Example 8.4.

Example 8.4
Flat major key signatures

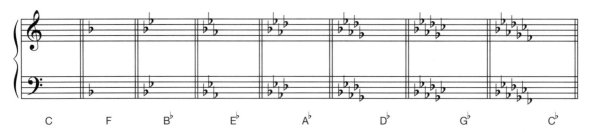

C   F   B♭   E♭   A♭   D♭   G♭   C♭

Hint for recognizing flat major key signatures: Like the previous tip for recognizing sharp keys, there are two easy ways to help recognize flat keys. The first method is to go down three **scale degrees** from the last **accidental**. Using this method, if D-flat is the last flat, go down first to C then B-flat (remember to include any flats in the key signature), and finally to A-flat. The second method is a bit more direct for two or more flats: except for the key of F major, the name of the flat key will be the second to last flat in the key signature. You will need to memorize that F has one flat (B-flat). This method is shown in Example 8.5.

Example 8.5
Recognizing flat major key signatures

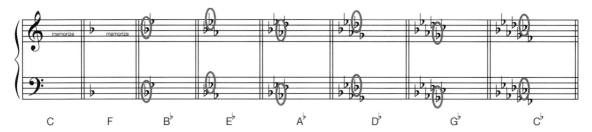

C   F   B♭   E♭   A♭   D♭   G♭   C♭

8.4 Minor Key Signatures

Since both **harmonic** and **melodic** minor scales add accidentals to alter the **natural** form, when writing music in minor keys the natural minor scale is used to form the key signature. The sharps and flats in minor key signatures are arranged in the exact same manner as for major keys, as shown in Example 8.6.

Example 8.6
Minor key signatures

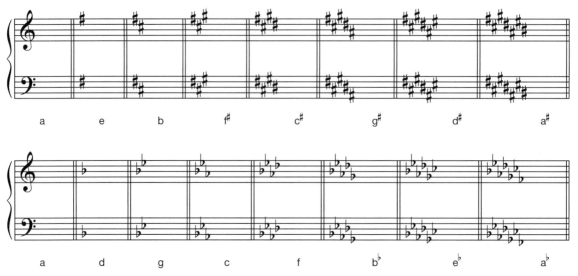

a   e   b   f♯   c♯   g♯   d♯   a♯

a   d   g   c   f   b♭   e♭   a♭

Hint for recognizing sharp minor key signatures: Most music composed in a minor key will make use of the harmonic or melodic minor scales, and therefore will have **chromatic** alterations within the music itself that fits those scales. Tonal melodies often end with the **tonic** as the final note. If the final note is not the tonic of the major key specified by the key signature, determine if it is scale degree 6. If so, the piece is most likely in minor on that tonic pitch. This is a very effective method of first determining if a piece is in major or minor. Once it is suspected that the passage is in minor, then the following hint is helpful in recognizing and/or confirming the key signature (until all minor key signatures are thoroughly memorized). **In sharp minor keys, the last sharp is one scale degree *above* tonic.** So, if there are two sharps in the key signature, the last sharp will be C-sharp. The scale degree below C-sharp is B, and the key signature is b minor. As with the major key signature hint, remember to include the sharp in the key signature (i.e. if E-sharp is the last sharp, the whole step below it is D-sharp, which is in the key signature). Notice that when referring to minor keys, a lower case **letter name** is used.

Hint for recognizing flat minor key signatures: For flat, minor keys, the hint for quick recognition is to **go up two scale degrees from the last flat**. If B-flat is the last flat, then up two scale degrees the pitch D, and d minor is the key. As always, remember to include the flats in the key signature, so if G-flat is the last flat, up to steps is the pitch B-flat, and the key is b-flat minor.

Summary of Hints

Note the pattern of up/down and increasing size:

- For major sharp keys: *Up **one** scale degree from the last sharp.*

- For minor sharp keys: *Down **one** scale degree from the last sharp.*

- For minor flat keys: *Up **two** scale degrees from the last flat.*

- For major flat keys: *Down **three** scale degrees from the last flat; or, the next to the last flat is the key.*

Of course, these are only temporary tools that should be used until all major and minor key signatures are completely memorized. But if the key signature is not immediately recognized, these tools can be helpful in avoiding errors and positively reinforcing the identification of the correct key.

8.5 Notating Key Signatures

Key signatures are always notated after the **clef** and before the **time signature** in common practice music. The key signature should appear at the beginning of every **staff** as long as that key is in effect. The order and spacing of the accidentals in the key signatures is very important, and in common practice music and modern music does not change.

Example 8.7
Key signature notation

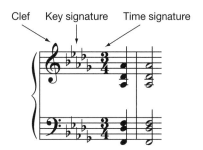

There are only two common exceptions in music notation regarding key signatures. In music written for the French horn, tradition has long dictated that no key signature is used, but rather, all accidentals are added individually. This custom, however, has been changing in recent years and now parts are often written for them using key signatures. Also, in jazz notation, it is customary to indicate the key signature only on the first staff **system** or when the key signature changes.

In scores that include a mixture of instruments, you may notice that sometimes there will be different key signatures for some of the staves. When the key signature is different for an instrument, it is because this is a **transposing instrument**. Because of the construction of the instrument, the music is written in one key, but the instrument sounds it in another. For many historical reasons, transposing instruments (mostly wind and brass instruments) have retained this process. Although you will see a variety of key signatures on the written score, all the instruments will *sound* in the same **key**.

Key Signatures for Alto and Tenor Clefs

The same principles apply to the use of key signatures in the **alto** and **tenor** clefs. The arrangement of sharps and flats is similar in the alto clef to those in the treble and bass clefs; however, the location of pitches in the tenor clef staff require a different arrangement of sharps in the key signature, as shown in Example 8.8.

Example 8.8
Key signatures for alto and tenor clefs

8.6 Relationships between Major and Minor Scales

There are two important relationships that exist between major and minor scales. The first is when both are related by use of the same key signature. This is called the **relative relationship**.

Notice that in each case in Example 8.9, the tonic of the relative minor key for any given major key is scale degree 6 in the major key. For example, in C major, scale degree 6 is "A," which is the relative minor of C major. The reverse also is true: scale degree 3 of any minor scale indicates the tonic of the relative major key. This strong relationship is frequently used in composing common practice music (Example 8.10).

Example 8.9

Relative major/minor key signature relationships

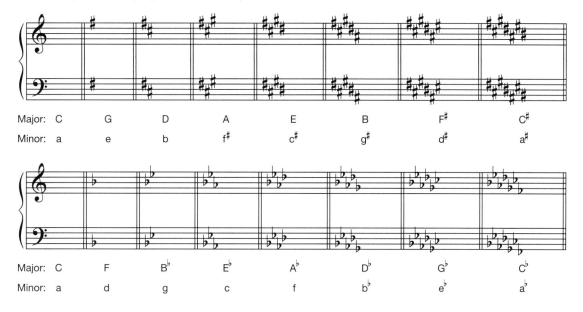

Major:	C	G	D	A	E	B	F#	C#
Minor:	a	e	b	f#	c#	g#	d#	a#

Major:	C	F	B♭	E♭	A♭	D♭	G♭	C♭
Minor:	a	d	g	c	f	b♭	e♭	a♭

 **Example 8.10**

Melody in C major moving to the relative minor (a minor)

The second important relationship between major and minor keys is the **parallel relationship**. In this relationship, both of the scales have the same tonic. C major is the parallel major of c minor, and vice-verse: c minor is the parallel minor of C major. This is also referred to as a **change of mode**, since only the *mode* of the scale (minor and major) changes, not the tonic. Both lines of Example 8.11 have "G" as tonic, but the mode has changed from minor to major.

 Example 8.11

Melody in G with parallel minor/major relationship

g minor

G major

Notice that in parallel relationships, the key signature will need to change (although if the passage is short enough, the composer will sometimes simply add **accidentals** to change the key). When there is a change in the key signature at the beginning of a new line of music, a **courtesy key signature** is added to the end of the previous staff line to help the performer recognize the change. When a courtesy key signature is added, the **barline** is moved in slightly to allow the needed space, and there is no barline following the last accidental. In **relative relationships**, both keys use the same key signature, so no change is necessary.

Parallel keys will always have a difference of three sharps or flats in their key signatures. The parallel minor key moves toward the flat side, so if the major key is a flat key, three flats are added to the key signature to create the parallel minor (i.e. B-flat major has two flats: $2 + 3 = 5$, so b-flat minor has five flats). If the major key is a sharp key, three sharps are subtracted (the equivalent of adding three flats, which cancel out the sharps) to determine the parallel minor key signature (i.e. B major has five sharps: $5 - 3 = 2$, so b minor has two sharps). For sharp keys with fewer than three sharps (as in Example 8.10), the number of sharps are first removed (each counting as one of the three accidentals that are changed) and then flats are added until there are a total of three changes in the key signature. For example, G major has one sharp. Taking away one sharp (1) then adding two flats (2) is a total of three changes. Another special case occurs in major keys with more than four flats, when adding three flats would result in a key signature with more than seven flats (i.e. D-flat major, with five flats, cannot form d-flat minor with eight flats). For these keys, the parallel minor is spelled enharmonically using sharps. So, for example, the parallel minor of D-flat major is c-sharp minor.

Summary of the relationships minor and major keys

- The RELATIVE relationship keeps the *same key signature*, but has a *different tonic*. The tonic of the relative minor is scale degree 6 of the relative major key. The tonic of the relative major is scale degree 3 of the minor scale.

- The PARALLEL relationship keeps *the same tonic*, but has a *different key signature*. Add three flats (or remove up to three sharps) to the major key signature to form the key signature of the parallel minor. Add three sharps (or remove three flats) to the minor key signature to form the key signature of the parallel major.

8.7 Memorizing Key Signatures

Memorizing all major and minor key signatures is an essential skill all musicians must master to both read and write tonal music. However, everyone learns best in a slightly different way. Some people find that simply memorizing a list of information (such as key signatures) is a simple task, while others have a very difficult time directly memorizing information and work best with some kind of memory "device" that helps them while they are memorizing the information. For this reason, each student should find the method that works best for them, and use it. If direct memorization is not your strongest method, the following sections present some helpful means to do so.

Using the order of the seven sharps in a **key signature** (which was memorized earlier in this chapter) leads to the creation of an easy tool to help you learn and memorize key signatures for all major and minor keys. If this order is not yet thoroughly memorized, it may be helpful to use the phrase below to remember the order:

F	C	G	D	A	E	B
Fat	*cats*	*go*	*down*	*alleys*	*eating*	*birds*

The Major Key Signature Tool

There can be a maximum of seven sharps or seven flats in a key signature. For major keys, the key of "C" has zero accidentals, the least possible, so put a zero after that letter:

F	C(0)	G	D	A	E	B

Now, add the following numbers above and below the letters. Start counting forward from the zero by adding a 1 above G, 2 above D, 3 above A, 4 above E, and 5 above B. Then loop back to the beginning of the line and add a 6 above F and a 7 above C. Below the numbers, count in the opposite direction, with a 1 below F, loop around to put a 2 below B, and so on until once again ending with a 7 below C:

6	7	1	2	3	4	5
F	C(0)	G	D	A	E	B
1	7	6	5	4	3	2

This final step is to add two lines between the numbers and letters: one from above F to above C, and another from below C to the end of the line (*easy hint*: remember to overlap the letter "C" since it has a seven both above and below):

"Sharp line"

6	7	1	2	3	4	5
F	C(0)	G	D	A	E	B
1	7	6	5	4	3	2

"Flat line"

The upper line is called the **Sharp line** and the lower line is called the **Flat line**. (This is easy to remember, since sharps *raise* notes and flats *lower* notes.)

Numbers next to a letter without a line between indicate the number of sharps (if above) or flats (if below) in that key signature. For example, the number 3 above "A" means there are three sharps in the key signature for A major. The number 1 below F indicates that in F major, there is one flat.

If a line is above or below a letter, then that indicates the **letter name** has a sharp key name (i.e. C-sharp) or a flat key name (i.e. G-flat) if below. The corresponding number of sharps or flats is the number on the other side of the line. So for A with a line below, it can easily be seen that A-flat major has four flats.

Example 8.12
The major key signature tool

	(F♯)	(C♯)					
Sharps:	6	7	1	2	3	4	5
	F	C(0)	G	D	A	E	B
Flats:	1	7	6	5	4	3	2
		(C♭)	(G♭)	(D♭)	(A♭)	(E♭)	(B♭)

The Minor Key Signature Tool

For creating the **Minor Key Signature Tool**, the same order of letters is used, but since the *Aeolian* mode is also the natural minor scale, the zero goes after the letter "A" instead of "C." The numbers and lines are added using the same process as before, this time beginning on "A," which has zero sharps or flats.

Example 8.13
The minor key signature tool

	(F♯)	(C♯)	(G♯)	(D♯)	(A♯)		
Sharps:	3	4	5	6	7	1	2
	F	C	G	D	A (0)	E	B
Flats:	4	3	2	1	7	6	5
					(A♭)	(E♭)	(B♭)

Follow the same procedure for reading the tool as before, and you will be able to quickly reference and practice naming all the minor key signatures. With a little practice, the **Key Signature Tools** for major and minor keys can be constructed in only a few seconds. Like all tools or hints, this is intended only as a starting point to help learn and memorize key signatures and to allow for the study music in all keys until the memorization process is complete. With time and practice, this goal of complete key mastery should be within anyone's reach.

The Circle of Fifths

A long-time traditional tool for memorizing major and minor key signatures that also shows the relative relationship is the **circle of fifths**. Using this diagram, each new sharp key is built upon the fifth scale degree of the previous key (located counterclockwise), which is how it got its name. **Enharmonic** key relationships are also shown by this device, which shows how G-flat and F-sharp major are related enharmonically. Major keys are listed on the outside of the circle, and the **relative minor key** is listed on the inside of the circle. This circular illustration also shows how **parallel minor keys** are always three changes counterclockwise and, conversely, the parallel major key signature is always three key signatures in the clockwise direction.

To create this tool, begin with 12 positions, just like a clock face. Start on C major/a minor (no sharps or flats) in the top, 12 o'clock position. To create the sharp keys, each key moving clockwise is scale degree 5 of the previous key (i.e. G is scale degree 5 in a C major scale). Proceed around to seven sharps. To create the flat keys, each key moving counterclockwise is scale degree 4 of the previous key. Proceed around to seven flats. To check your accuracy, the keys with five, six, and seven sharps and flats should be **enharmonically equivalent** to each other.

Although more complex than the Key Signature Tools, some may find it a useful tool in memorizing key signatures, and because of its long history all musicians should be aware of it.

Example 8.14
The circle of fifths

Major Keys

Minor Keys

Chapter Summary

Key signatures are specific arrangements of sharps or flats that indicate all of the **chromatic alterations** (**accidentals**) used in a key. Key signatures are always written after the **clef** and before the **time signature** in each **staff system** in which that key is in effect, except in jazz notation. A **courtesy key signature** is used at the end of a staff when there is a change in the key signature at the beginning of the following system.

Sharp keys have between one and seven sharps, and **flat keys** have between one and seven flats. The keys of C major and a minor have no sharps or flats. Both major and minor keys make use of all of the above key signatures. Major and minor keys have two principal relationships: **Relative keys** are those having the same number of sharps or flats in their key signatures. The relative minor is always the scale built upon scale degree 6 in the relative major. **Parallel keys** are those having the same **tonic** but different modes (major and minor), and therefore have different key signatures. All parallel keys have key signatures that are three sharps or flats apart. Minor keys have three more flats/fewer sharps than their parallel major keys.

Although there are many hints and techniques for recognizing and writing key signatures, it is essential that all musicians thoroughly memorize all major and minor key signatures. Until this happens, the **Key Signature Tool** and the **Circle of Fifths** are two helpful tools to aid in memorizing key signatures.

Rhythmic Reading: Triplets

1 Practice the following until you are able to smoothly and evenly change between eighth notes and the triplets, then read the following two exercises.

a)

b)

2 Practice the following taking care to make a distinct difference between the quarter-eighth triplet figures and the dotted eight-sixteenth figures. Once mastered, then read the following two exercises.

a)

b)

Chapter 8 Exercises

1   Provide the Major Key and Key Signature for the following passages:

a)   KEY: _____   KEY SIGNATURE

b)   KEY: _____   KEY SIGNATURE

c)   KEY: _____   KEY SIGNATURE

d)   KEY: _____   KEY SIGNATURE

2   Write the full, correct, seven-sharp key signature in both clefs in each measure (if by the end it is not memorized and you are unable to write it automatically with little thought, continue on blank staff paper until it is mastered):

3   Write the full, correct, seven-flat key signature in both clefs in each measure (if by the end it is not memorized and you are unable to write it automatically with little thought, continue on blank staff paper until it is mastered):

You should be as comfortable writing your key signatures as you are writing your own signature. Continue practicing until you can notate seven sharps or flats in both staves in less than 15 seconds.

4 Fill in the blanks:

   a) What is the order of sharps in the key signature?

   _____

   b) What is a hint for recognizing major SHARP keys?

   _____

   c) What is a hint for recognizing minor SHARP keys?

   _____

   d) What is a hint for recognizing major FLAT keys?

   _____

   e) What is a hint for recognizing minor FLAT keys?

   _____

5 In the space below draw the requested Key Signature Tool:

   a) Major Key Signature Tool:

   b) Minor Key Signature Tool:

6 Write the full, correct, seven SHARP key signature in each measure below (refer to Example 8.8 in the text for correct positioning):

7 Write the MAJOR key signatures below as requested. Try not to use the Key
Signature Tool in question 6, but confirm your answer before writing it down:

a) D major   **b)** E major   **c)** B major   **d)** D♭ major   **e)** C♯ major   **f)** C♭ major

8 Identify the key as quickly as possible without looking at the above tools unless
needed (M = Major; m = minor key):

a) m:3 sharps_____   **b)** M:6 flats_____   **c)** m:3 flats_____

d) M:4 flats_____   **e)** M:5 sharps _____   **f)** m:6 flats _____

g) M:5 flats _____   **h)** m:5 flats_____

9 Notate the following MAJOR key signatures in both staves as requested. If you
don't remember the correct key within 3–4 seconds, refer back to the Key
Signature Tools on the previous page, determine the correct key and repeat it out
loud five or more times before writing the key signature:

a) B   **b)** A   **c)** F   **d)** C   **e)** E   **f)** E♭   **g)** D   **h)** F

i) G   **j)** B♭   **k)** A♭   **l)** C♭   **m)** D♭   **n)** C♯

10 Notate the following MINOR key signatures in both staves as requested, using the same rules as above:

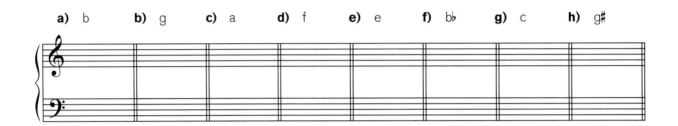

a) b   **b)** g   **c)** a   **d)** f   **e)** e   **f)** b♭   **g)** c   **h)** g♯

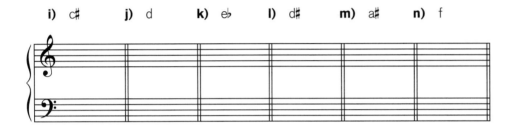

i) c♯   **j)** d   **k)** e♭   **l)** d♯   **m)** a♯   **n)** f

11 Fill in the blanks:

a) The parallel major of *g minor* is: _____

b) The parallel minor of *C major* is: _____

c) The parallel major of *b-flat minor* is: _____

d) The relative minor of *B major* is: _____

e) The relative major of *f minor* is: _____

12 Draw the circle of fifths chart below (optional).

CHAPTER 9

Aural Application: Sight Singing

Many students have learned to sight sing music by using **solfege** as part of their choir experience. Solfege is a method of assigning Latin syllables to each **scale degree** that was developed in the middle of the eleventh century by a monk and music teacher called **Guido d'Arezzo**. Based on the chant *Ut queant laxis*, also known commonly as the *Hymn of St. Joannes*, it was used to help teach monks to sing chant.

Example 9.1
The origin of solfege: *Ut queant laxis* (*Hymn of St. Joannes*)

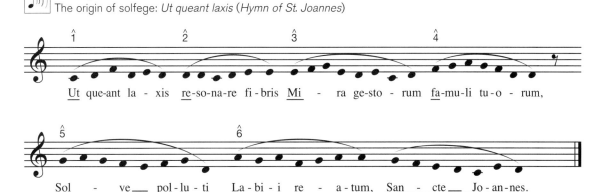

The syllables **ut—re—mi—fa—sol—la** became the standard means of referring to scale degrees 1 to 6. For scale degree 7, which is not used in this hymn or many chants of that period, the syllable **si** was derived from the initials for *Saint Joannes* (in Latin, a "J" becomes an "I"). These syllables are used even today in many European countries to refer to the pitches C—D—E—F—G—A—B rather than letters. Over the centuries, as these were translated and used by more and more musicians to learn singing, the syllable **do** was substituted for **ut**, and **ti** was substituted for **si**.

From these basic solfege syllables, **chromatic inflections** were added to allow for singing music with **accidentals**. These inflections, like sharps and flats, raise or lower the basic **diatonic** syllable and are listed in Example 9.2. Like so many things in music, traditions endure, and this system of singing continues to be used even today by many music schools around the world. There are also other methods of learning to sight sing music. Besides singing on a neutral syllable (such as "la"), two basic approaches are used: fixed systems relating a number, letter or syllable to a given **pitch class**, and movable systems, where numbers or syllables are assigned to notes based upon scale degrees. The following lists the most common systems in the order in which they are presented in this text, and your instructor will guide you in which system is used for your class.

Fixed Do Solfege (with or without inflections)

- Pitch class letter names (fixed, with or without inflections)
- Movable do major
- La-based minor
- Do-based minor
- Scale degree numbers

Each system has its strengths and weaknesses, and no system is perfect. All are simply a means to an end: to be able to accurately read, understand, hear internally, and sing music at sight. Regardless of which system is used, a basic familiarity with all of them is helpful, as this knowledge will not only provide an alternate approach that may work better for an individual melody or student, but also will provide a means of better communicating with musicians from other schools and/or those who speak other languages who have learned one of these methods.

9.1 Fixed Do Solfege

Since the syllables for solfege in the key of C major are also used in many non-English languages as the names of the pitch classes (rather than letter names A, B, C, etc.), many non-English-speaking parts of the world teach sight singing using **fixed do solfege**. In this system, C is always "do," D is always "re," and so forth, regardless of the **key** or **octave** in which one is singing.

Example 9.2
Fixed do solfege

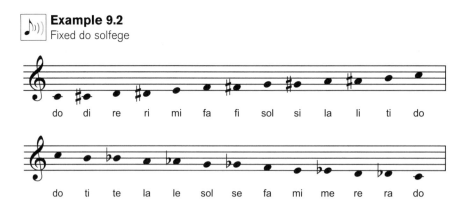

This has the benefit of being simple to learn and also can help in developing the ability to fluently read music in all **clefs** and to aurally recognize specific pitch classes away from a **keyboard** or another pitch reference. This ability is often called **perfect pitch** or **absolute pitch**. When one is able to recognize pitches in relation to a given pitch, this is called **relative pitch**.

In many European systems of sight singing, the uninflected syllables (do, re, mi, fa, sol, la, si) only are used and students must aurally raise or lower the pitch a half step to accommodate accidentals. This would be the equivalent of reading the letter names in English.

9.2 Pitch Class Letter Names

A second fixed system of sight singing used in English-speaking schools is by just singing the **pitch class letter names**. This system has the advantage of reinforcing the reading of pitches in any clef, and direct application to the way one performs and discusses music in general. Since the addition of an accidental adds syllables, some schools sing only the letter name and omit pronouncing the accidental in rapid passages.

Example 9.3
Letter names (fixed)

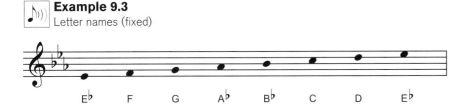

E♭   F   G   A♭   B♭   C   D   E♭

9.3 "Movable Do" Solfege for Major Keys

Movable do solfege is based on the functional relationships between scale degrees, not the **specific pitches** themselves. This system treats **tonic** as "do" no matter what the key, and transposes the other syllables to match the scale degrees above tonic, as shown in Table 9.1. Chromatic inflections are added exactly as in fixed do solfege, and these inflections are similarly transposed.

Table 9.1 Diatonic movable do solfege

Scale degree number	$\hat{1}$	$\hat{2}$	$\hat{3}$	$\hat{4}$	$\hat{5}$	$\hat{6}$	$\hat{7}$
Scale degree name	Tonic	Supertonic	Mediant	Sub-dominant	Dominant	Sub-mediant	Leading tone
Solfege	Do	Re	Mi	Fa	Sol	La	Ti

The advantage of this system is that it allows one to hear music functionally: "sol" is always the dominant, "ti" is always the leading tone, and "fi" is always the raised fourth scale degree. This makes the visual and aural recognition of how notes function more apparent and aids in discussing principles of music theory. For this reason, it is used in many music schools.

9.4 Movable Solfege for Minor Scales

When singing in minor keys, there are two forms of movable solfege that are commonly used along with Movable Do solfege for major keys, and they reflect the **relative** and **parallel** relationships discussed in the **previous chapter**. Both have their strengths and applicability, and so both are commonly used. Both, however, are only used in conjunction with Movable Do major solfege, not with fixed or number systems.

La-based minor **solfege** is based on the **relative minor relationship** to major keys. The **natural minor scale** in a relative minor begins on scale degree 6 (which would be "la" in the relative major). In **harmonic** and **melodic** minor scale forms, note how scale degrees 6 and 7 are altered according to the standard inflections for those scale degrees in Example 9.4.

Example 9.4
La-based minor solfege

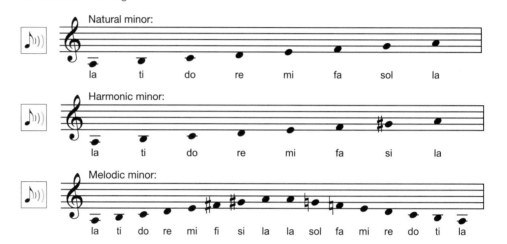

This system is very effective for melodies that move to the relative major and/or back again, since there is then no need to change any of the syllables or relationships between syllables. Since many examples of such melodies occur in **common practice** music (and in the commercial music of today), this system is taught in many high school choral programs in the United States. Notice how la-based minor solfege functions in Example 9.5.

Example 9.5
La-minor melody moving to the relative major

A weakness of the la-based minor system is that the functional relationships between syllables in minor are completely different from those in major, and even conflict with them: in major "sol" is the **dominant** and "mi" is the **mediant**, while in minor "mi" is the dominant and "do" is the mediant.

Do-based minor solfege is based on the **parallel minor relationship** to major keys. In this system, tonic is always "do," the dominant is always "sol" and the functionality of these and other important scale degrees remains the same as in major keys. The changes in solfege are only between those scale degrees that change between major and minor: scale degrees 3, 6, and 7, which are inflected according to the list in Example 9.2. The Do-based minor solfege system for all three minor scale forms is shown in Example 9.6.

Example 9.6
Do-minor solfege

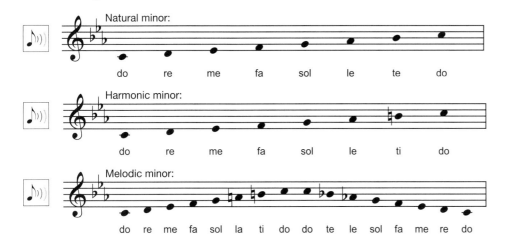

Because the functionality of the scale degrees remains the same in both major and minor, and the raised scale degrees 6 and 7 in melodic minor are the same syllables as in the major scale, this system is very popular in college-level music theory courses. It is also very helpful when singing melodies that change between major and minor modes using the parallel key relationship.

Example 9.7
Do-based minor–major melody

9.5 Scale Degree Numbers

Singing using **scale degree** numbers works the same in both major and minor keys. The scale degree number is sung without inflection. This helps reinforce the study of written theory and function, but also means that a different pitch is sung on the same syllable for scale degrees 3, 6, and 7 depending on the scale type. When singing the numbers, seven is often shortened to *se'n* so that it is only one syllable.

Example 9.8
Scale degree numbers

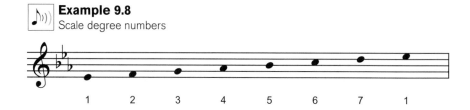

9.6 Application

All these are popular and commonly used systems. In any system, it is important to first determine the key and range of the example and **tonally index** the passage. **Indexing** is the visual and aural identification of tonic, dominant, and other scale degrees. It also involves determining the syllable or number for each note using whatever system is in place. This allows one to be able to *read* the passage rather than have to calculate it note by note. In fixed systems, the syllable is consistent, so recognition is not the challenge: the challenge is hearing and knowing the correct pitch and function associated with that syllable. In movable systems, the ear and eye must reorient to the particular **key**, assigning the correct pitch and syllable to each note used. As a frame of reference while singing, the **tonic** needs to be well established. To accomplish this, prior to singing a passage the tonic pitch should be given, and then a scale or other pattern sung that orients the ear to that key. Example 9.9 shows a **tonicization pattern** which may be sung to help quickly accomplish this. As singing this or any pattern, the student should simultaneously be looking at the appropriate line or space for that pitch so that both the visual and aural identity of each note is established before attempting to sing the passage. Then the goal becomes to simply remember this information and read the passage, not to calculate it.

Example 9.9
Sample tonicization patterns for D major and minor

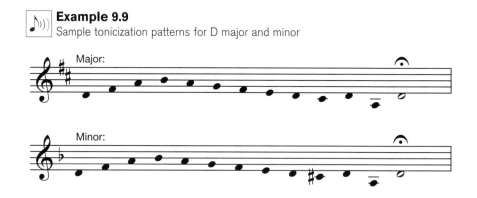

The important principle is to master one system well enough to be able to use it fluently, and to be familiar with other systems so that you can work well with musicians who have learned those. Your instructor will help determine which system is used for your class.

Chapter Summary

Singing music at sight is aided by a consistent approach and method. Modern systems use **pitch class letter names**, **scale degrees**, and *solfege*—a historic approach used since the eleventh century. There are two principal approaches using solfege syllables: **Fixed Do** assigns syllables to pitch classes regardless of mode, key or function, and is especially useful for musicians with, or those who aspire to develop, **perfect pitch**. Since the pitches are absolute, it is equally effective for major, minor or even non-tonal music. **Movable Do** transposes "do" to the **tonic**, assigning the same syllables as in fixed do to **scale degrees** rather than fixed pitch classes, allowing for ease of **transposition** and easier visual and aural recognition of how notes function when discussing principles of music theory.

In minor keys, **movable La minor** uses the **relative minor relationship** between major and minor keys, creating a system more consistent to the key signature, while **movable Do minor** retains the functionality and commonality of scale degrees 1, 2, 4, and 5 between major and minor, and like the **parallel relationship**, alters only scale degrees 3, 6, and 7.

Tonal indexing is the visual and aural assignment of pitch and syllable to the notes to be sung. This can be best accomplished by singing a scale or other **tonicization pattern** prior to attempting to sing a passage.

All systems have their merits, and your instructor will guide you in which system will be used for your class. However, since musicians use all of these systems, a basic familiarity with all of them is essential to professionally communicate with others about music.

Chapter 9 Exercises

1   Tonicization

Using the system chosen by your instructor, sing one of these two patterns, or another of your instructor's choosing, prior to any passage in C major. If singing in a clef other than treble, visualize the position of each note on the lines and spaces for that clef as you sing the pattern. Accuracy first: then speed.

2   Exercises in C Major with Step-wise Motion

With all sight singing, first sing the tonicization pattern, then *silently* scan the example to catch any areas of possible difficulty. After tonicizing, do not make any sound until your first attempt: you only get one try at sight singing—anything after that is *practice*. When truly sight singing, give yourself one measure of beats, then *sing all the way through in tempo without stopping*. Do not attempt to "correct mistakes"—that is for practice. After you sight sing a passage, *then* go back, sing it over and over and practice until it is solidly mastered. Strive toward reading the music rather than calculating it.

3 Tonicization for C Minor

4 Exercises in C Minor with Step-wise Motion

Sight sing, then practice as with major.

a)

b)

c)

d)

e)

f)

Speed Test #1:

Practice each of these for accuracy first, then work up to as fast as possible. You may need to start at a sixteenth-note pulse, but should eventually memorize and work up to a moderato quarter-note pulse. This will help you build the muscle memory and fluency in using whatever system you are using. This process will likely take some time. Practice daily with gradual increments in tempo until it is up to speed.

a) Major

b) Minor

CHAPTER 10

Intervals

10.1 Types of Intervals

An **interval** is the distance between two pitches. Any interval can be measured horizontally when two pitches are sounded in succession over time (rhythm) or vertically when two or more pitches are sounded at the same time. Horizontally occurring intervals may be either ascending or descending and are often referred to as **melodic intervals**. Vertical intervals are always measured as the distance above the lower note and are often referred to as **harmonic intervals**.

Example 10.1
Melodic and harmonic intervals

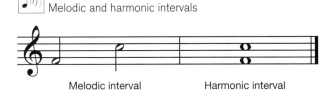

Melodic interval   Harmonic interval

In Example 10.1, both intervals are between the same two pitches, so they are the same size regardless of whether they are melodic (ascending or descending) or harmonic. No matter how the two notes are arranged, the distance remains the same, and therefore the interval remains the same and is described using the same term. This principle is especially helpful when identifying interval size.

10.2 General Intervals

General intervals (also sometimes referred to as "generic intervals" or "**interval numbers**") are a means of measuring distance between two notes derived from the distances between **scale degrees**. By treating the lower note as **tonic** (scale degree 1), a general interval uses the scale degree above that note to determine the interval size. The general interval between two notes that occupy the same line or space is called a **unison**. Moving upward through the scale degrees, the distance between scale degree 1 and scale degree 2 is a **second**. Scale degree 3 is a **third** above tonic, scale degree 4 is a **fourth** above tonic, and so on until the octave, as shown in Example 10.2. The term **octave** is used rather than "eighth" since it returns to scale degree 1 and there is no "eighth scale degree." When determining general intervals, **accidentals** in the **key signature** and **chromatic** alterations are not considered—only the general size of the interval is considered.

Example 10.2
General intervals

Since accidentals are not considered when measuring general intervals, any and all combinations of accidentals on either note of the examples in Table 10.1 belong to the same **general interval** category (seconds, thirds, etc.). In these examples, notice how the visual space between the notes remains the same, regardless of what accidentals are present. This can be a great help in quickly identifying or writing an interval.

General intervals are especially useful when discussing the basic characteristics of music. Consistent use of only a few general intervals in a melody can help it to have a sense of unity and identity. Earlier, the **rhythmic reduction** of the melody from the first movement of **Mozart's** Symphony No. 40 revealed his use of only a few **rhythmic motives**. When analyzing the general intervals used in this enduring melody, it is interesting to note that Mozart also only uses a few general intervals: **unisons** (u), **seconds** (2), and **sixths** (6). Notice also how the second half of this example uses 100 percent the same general intervals and rhythm as the first half, which helps to create the aural relationship that is so prominent in this famous passage.

Example 10.3
General intervals (melodic) used in Mozart, Symphony No. 40, Mvt. I, mm. 1–8

Table 10.1 Visual recognition of general intervals

Unisons		Both occupy the same line or space. Although the noteheads are next to one another, they sound at the same time. Accidentals (if present) always come in pairs, with the first accidental belonging to the left notehead, and the second belonging to the right notehead.
Seconds		Both are on adjacent lines and spaces. The lower note is always to the *left* of the upper note and stem. In performance, both sound at the same time.
Thirds		Both are on lines or both are on spaces with no gaps between. These are some of the easiest to recognize.
Fourths		One larger than a third. If one note is on a line, then the other will be on a space with a small gap between (one space).
Fifths		Both are on lines or both are on spaces with one line or space gap between them. Twice the size of a third.
Sixths		One larger than a fifth. Like fourths, if one note is on a line the other must be on a space. There will be a two-space gap between the notes.
Sevenths		Both are on lines or both are on spaces with a large gap of two or three spaces between. One less than an octave.
Octaves		This is a very common interval that must be visually memorized. If one note is on a line, then the other will be on a space.

10.3 Specific Intervals (Diatonic)

Although the use of the general interval of a second in each half of Example 10.3 is identical, a closer examination reveals that the number of **half steps** between all but the final of the **seconds** differ. Although general intervals provide a means to discuss music in general terms, and allow for the aural recognition of basic motivic relationships, a more specific means of defining intervals is needed for further **analysis** and understanding of the details in music. **Specific intervals** are exact sizes as measured in **half steps**. Like a one-foot ruler, which has 12 inches, each octave has 12 half steps, and these are used to measure interval size. Anything smaller than a half step is called a

microtone and was not used in common practice music. The names of specific intervals are derived from a combination of the **general interval number** plus a prefix that defines the interval's **quality**. The most common specific intervals are **perfect**, **major**, and **minor** intervals.

Perfect intervals (Table 10.2) are those that remain the same in both major and minor scales, and that if altered by even a half step in either direction fundamentally change in their sound and quality. The perfect intervals are the perfect **unison** (zero half steps apart), perfect **fourth** (five half steps apart), perfect **fifth** (seven half steps apart) and the perfect **octave** (12 half steps apart).

Table 10.2 Perfect intervals

Perfect interval	Number of half steps	Audio example
Perfect unison (PU)	0	🎵
Perfect fourth (P4)	5	🎵
Perfect fifth (P5)	7	🎵
Perfect octave (P8)	12	🎵

For the remaining general interval categories, each has two versions a half step apart that sound related. These are given the prefix "**major**" (from the Latin meaning "greater" or "larger") and "**minor**" (from the Latin meaning "lesser" or "smaller"). All major intervals are a half step larger than their corresponding minor interval. **Major intervals** are abbreviated by using a capitol "M" before the general interval number, and **minor intervals** use a lower case "m" as their abbreviation. Table 10.3 lists all of the major and minor intervals with the number of half steps each contains.

Table 10.3 Major and minor intervals

Perfect interval	Number of half steps	Audio example
Minor second (m2)	1	🎵
Major second (M2)	2	🎵
Minor third (m3)	3	🎵
Major third (M3)	4	🎵
Minor sixth (m6)	8	🎵
Major sixth (M6)	9	🎵
Minor seventh (m7)	10	🎵
Major seventh (M7)	11	🎵

Notice that any time a major interval is reduced by a half step, it becomes a minor type. Also, when comparing the Tables 10.2 and 10.3, there is one specific interval missing: that which contains six half steps. This interval is generically called the **tritone** (meaning three "tones" or whole steps). Adding this unique interval to the previous two tables results in the following list of the most commonly found specific intervals and the number of half steps in each. Notice that except for the m2 and tritone, all of these intervals exist as **diatonic** scale degrees in either the **major** or **natural minor** scales using the lower note (C) as tonic. In this case, the m3, m6, and m7 belong to the c minor scale, and the M3, M6, and M7 belong to the C major scale.

 Example 10.4
Perfect, major, and minor intervals up to an octave

Unison	m2	M2	m3	M3	P4	Tritone	P5	m6	M6	m7	M7	P8
0	1	2	3	4	5	6	7	8	9	10	11	12

10.4 Chromatic Alterations of Intervals

Although Example 10.4 covers all perfect, major, and minor intervals above tonic in a singular, systematic manner, composers frequently chromatically alter these diatonic intervals to form additional specific intervals. Consider a familiar interval from the **harmonic minor scale**:

 Example 10.5
The harmonic minor scale

The interval between the A-flat and the B-natural has *three* half steps: one more than a major second. When an interval is enlarged by one half step beyond its normal major or perfect state, it is called an **augmented** interval, usually indicated with a plus sign or the prefix "Aug" (i.e. an augmented second is notated by the symbols +2 or **Aug2**). Since the interval of A-flat to B-flat is a major second (two half steps), when it is enlarged by adding the B-natural, it becomes an **augmented second**. This is true of all major and perfect intervals: when they are chromatically enlarged (or literally "**augmented**") by one half step by either lowering the bottom note or raising the top note, they become augmented. Notice that this only occurs when the **letter names** of both notes are not changed: if in the above example, the A-flat were **enharmonically** changed to be a G-sharp, the general interval would no longer be a second, it would be a third. The **tendency** of the A-flat is to resolve down to the G-natural. If it were respelled as a G-sharp, it would have a tendency to resolve up to an A-natural. Composers are usually very careful to spell pitches as they function. This is a prime reason why it is important not to enharmonically respell notes. The following is an example of two ways to expand a perfect fifth into an augmented fifth—the first by raising the upper note, the second by lowering the bottom note.

Example 10.6
Augmenting an interval

When a minor or perfect interval is reduced by a half step, it becomes a **diminished** interval, normally indicated with a superscript circle sign or the prefix "dim" (i.e. a diminished second is notated by the symbols **°2** or **dim2**). The same principles apply as for **augmented** intervals: the **general interval** must remain the same. The diminished quality is obtained by **chromatically** lowering the upper note or raising the bottom note.

 Example 10.7
Diminishing an interval

It is also possible—although it is very rarely done—to chromatically expand an augmented interval by a half step. This would create a **doubly augmented interval**. Equally rare, yet possible, is the **doubly diminished interval**, which is chromatically reduced from a diminished interval by a half step. Discussion of these advanced intervals will be reserved for later theory studies.

Example 10.8 summarizes the basic relationship between all intervals, via chromatic alteration by half-steps.

Example 10.8
Relationships between specific interval qualities

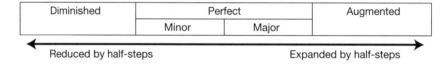

Diminished	Perfect		Augmented
	Minor	Major	

Reduced by half-steps ←———————————→ Expanded by half-steps

- Perfect intervals reduce into diminished and expand into augmented

- Major intervals reduce into minor and expand into augmented

- Minor intervals reduce into diminished and expand into major

- Diminished intervals expand into minor for seconds, thirds, sixths, and sevenths, or perfect for unisons, fourths, fifths, and octaves

- Augmented intervals reduce into major for seconds, thirds, sixths, and sevenths, or perfect for unisons, fourths, fifths, and octaves

10.5 Writing and Recognizing Specific Intervals

When being asked to recognize or write **specific intervals**, there are two steps that will help you to avoid common errors. First, identify the **general interval** size, then identify the interval's specific **quality**. The general interval is based solely on the number of scale degrees/letter names between the notes. The interval's quality (perfect, major, minor, augmented, diminished, etc.) is based on the number of half steps it contains.

Identifying Specific Intervals using Chromatic Counting

It is essential that all musicians are able to count the number of half steps between any two notes quickly. The **chromatic scale** is the fastest means of doing this. Using the fingerings for your instrument or on the musical keyboard, practice chromatic scales until you can easily play an octave up or down, beginning on any pitch, in less than 2–3 seconds. Besides being an essential skill for performance and sight reading, this will also allow you to determine the number of half steps between any two notes very quickly. It may be helpful to "air-jam" while doing this, as your muscle memory on your instrument or the piano will allow you to count more quickly than mentally spelling each half step. For example, if you were asked to determine the specific interval between E-flat up to D-flat, first identify it as the **general interval** of a **seventh**, then count half steps (10) to determine the **quality**.

Example 10.9
Chromatic counting of specific intervals

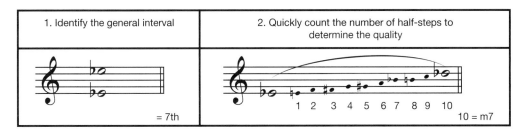

1. Identify the general interval	2. Quickly count the number of half-steps to determine the quality

Identifying Specific Intervals using Scales

Counting half steps does require that the number of half steps in each specific interval is thoroughly memorized. For some intervals, particularly smaller ones, this method works quite well. However, if you have thoroughly memorized your scales and key signatures, the following method may work better for most common intervals. First, recognize the general interval. Then, treating the lower note of the interval as tonic, determine if the upper note of the interval matches the corresponding scale degree for either the major or natural minor scale built on the lower note. **Perfect fourths** and **fifths** fit both major and minor keys. **Seconds** may be recognized as whole (M2) or half (m2) steps. If the others fit the major scale/key, then the interval quality is major. If it fits the natural minor scale/key, then it is minor. As key signatures and scales are more thoroughly memorized and used, this process becomes very quick and direct for most musicians. Example 10.10 demonstrates this for C major and c minor.

Example 10.10
Identifying specific intervals via major and minor scales

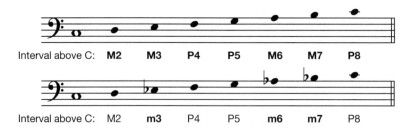

This allows for the fast identification and writing of commonly found **diatonic intervals**, but will not immediately identify intervals above pitches that do not have a normal key (G-flat minor, for example), or for **augmented, diminished, doubly augmented**, and **doubly diminished** intervals. However, when combined with the following method of relating an unknown interval to a known interval, even these less commonly found intervals can be simple to determine.

Identifying Unknown Specific Intervals via Relation to Known Intervals

Once you begin identifying intervals, you will find yourself recognizing some at sight. Or, using the scale/key recognition method, you may be able to quickly determine some intervals but not others. For unknown intervals that are similar to your recognized intervals, the chart of basic interval **quality** relationships can be used to quickly determine the unknown interval by relating it to a known interval.

Example 10.11
Half step relationships between interval qualities

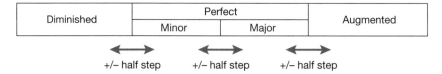

By mentally adding or subtracting one or more half steps to or from the unknown interval, you may find that it becomes a known interval. Then, using the above relationships, you can determine the original interval. A M3 reduced by a half step become a m3. A P4 reduced by a half step becomes a °4. A M6 reduced by two half steps becomes a °6. This method works for all recognized intervals. For instance, if you are asked for the specific interval for B-flat up to F-sharp, you may not immediately recognize this interval, but you may remember that F is part of the B-flat major scale, and therefore B-flat to *F-natural* is a perfect fifth. Since the sharp on the F increases (augments) the size of the interval by a half step, this creates an interval a half step larger than a perfect fifth: an augmented fifth.

Example 10.12
Relating unknown intervals to known intervals

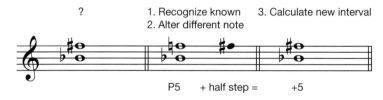

A second method of using closely related intervals is useful when the *lower* note does not fit a common key, B-double flat, for example. Although there is no major or minor scale built on B-double flat, B-flat major and minor are common and simple scales. If you are asked for the interval of B-double flat up to F-flat (Example 10.13), this may seem daunting, but when *both* pitches are raised a **chromatic half step** (don't change the letter name!) the space between them remains the same and it is simple to see that B-flat up to F-natural is a perfect fifth. By transposing both notes by the same amount (usually up or down a chromatic half step) a more simple, recognizable interval is often formed.

Example 10.13
Relating unknown intervals to known intervals

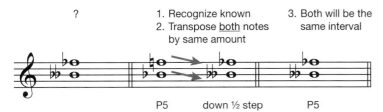

As you learn to immediately recognize more and more intervals, you will also be able to quickly figure out the closely related intervals based on small chromatic alterations to them, and soon you can quickly identify most intervals without having to count half steps between the pitches.

10.6 Melodic Intervals

In any melodic passage of music there will typically be a variety of intervals. From any given note in the music, the next note will either be higher, lower, or the same. Since intervals are the same distance apart whether measured from top note to bottom, or bottom note to top, melodic intervals are calculated the same way whether ascending upward or descending downward: a second below is the same distance as a second above, and a sixth below is the same distance as a sixth above.

Example 10.14
Identifying melodic general intervals

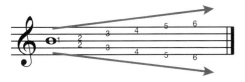

Identifying **melodic** general intervals is done in the same way as for **harmonic intervals**. It may help to visualize the notes one over another to more clearly see the spatial relationship.

Identifying melodic specific intervals is also done via the same processes as for harmonic intervals. For all intervals, remember to first identify the **general interval**, then to identify the interval **quality**.

10.7 Simple and Compound Intervals

Simple intervals are those with a general interval less than or equal to an **octave**. Intervals an octave and larger are termed **compound intervals**. Compound means something is made up of more than one part and, in this case, it means one or more octaves plus an interval. If an octave is thought of as the "eighth scale degree," one step larger (an octave plus a second) would form a **ninth**, and scale degree 3 (an octave plus a third) above that would be a **tenth**, and so on. When analyzing more advanced examples, it sometimes becomes important to recognize intervals between a ninth and a **thirteenth**, and to retain their function as such without reduction to their "octave plus . . ." identity. Example 10.15 shows these common compound general intervals. Compound specific intervals are determined just like their simple counterparts, counting scale degrees above the lower note.

Example 10.15
Common general compound intervals

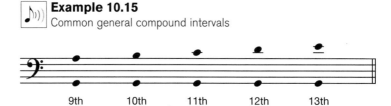

In analyzing common practice music, an octave is often reduced to a unison via the principle of **octave equivalence** (discussed in **Chapter 3**). In these cases, compound intervals are frequently reduced to **simple intervals** by lowering the top note to within an octave of the lower note. For example, listen to the intervals in Example 10.16 and notice how the second interval in each case sounds aurally related and similar to the first.

Example 10.16
Relationships between compound intervals and their reduced versions

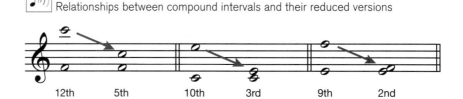

To find the equivalent simple **general interval** for any **compound interval**, subtract seven from the compound interval for the first octave, and eight for each additional octave it contains. For example in the first interval in Example 10.16:

$$12 - 7 = 5$$

a twelfth reduces to a **fifth.**

If the upper note were a C6 instead of a C5, the compound interval would be a twentieth (notice how cumbersome that would be!). By subtracting 15 (7 + 8), it reduces to a simple **fifth**—which is much easier to work with.

If you are not mathematically inclined, compound intervals may be reduced to their simple equivalent by lowering the top note or raising the bottom note by one or more octaves until the two are within an octave, then visually identifying the interval.

Specific compound intervals have the same interval **quality** as their simple reductions: a M9 is a M2 plus an octave; an Aug11 is an Aug4 plus an octave; and so forth.

10.8 Inversion of Intervals

The principle of **octave equivalence** creates another relationship between certain intervals. In any simple interval, if the bottom note is raised an octave, or the top note is lowered an octave, as shown in the second line of Example 10.17, a new interval is formed, called an **inversion** of the first interval. This—like reduced compound intervals—has an obvious aural relationship to the original interval.

Example 10.17
Relationships between intervals and their inversions

Notice the symmetrical relationship between general intervals that **inversion** forms around the interval of a **tritone**.

- All octaves invert into unisons
- All seconds invert into sevenths
- All thirds invert into sixths
- All fourths invert into fifths

- All unisons invert into octaves
- All sevenths invert into seconds
- All sixths invert into thirds
- All fifths invert into fourths

The following shows how general intervals invert:

Example 10.18
Inversional relationships of general intervals

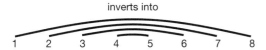

There is also a simple mathematical relationship that **inverts** general intervals: subtract the general interval's number from nine and you have the inversion. So, to invert a seventh:

$$9 - 7 = 2$$

a seventh inverts into a second

There is also an interesting symmetrical relationship between the interval qualities that also forms around the tritone:

- All perfect intervals invert into a perfect interval
- All major intervals invert into a minor interval
- All minor intervals invert into a major interval
- All diminished intervals invert into an augmented interval
- All augmented intervals invert into a diminished interval.

Our earlier chart can also be used to illustrate this relationship very clearly:

Example 10.19
Inversional relationships of interval qualities

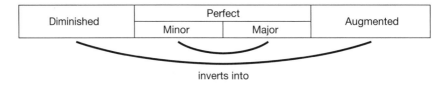

Once again, a simple mathematical subtraction can be used to invert **specific intervals**. By subtracting the number of half steps from 12, the number of half steps of the inversion can be found. So, for inverting a minor seventh:

A minor seventh = 10 half steps

12 − 10 = 2

A second with two half-steps is a major second

Remember: you must first invert the general interval (seventh into a second) and then use the number of half steps to only determine the **quality**, not changing the general interval. This becomes particularly important when dealing with **augmented** and **diminished** intervals.

Identifying Specific Intervals using Inversions

For larger intervals, the principle of **inversion** can be helpful in identifying the specific interval size. Example 10.20 demonstrates this method using the pitches F-sharp and E-flat. When the F-sharp is inverted (raised an octave so that it is above the E-flat), it is a simple matter to determine that it is a second with three half steps, or an augmented second. Seconds invert into sevenths, and augmented intervals invert into diminished intervals, so the original interval must be a diminished seventh. Since smaller intervals may be easier for some to identify, inverting the interval, then identifying the smaller resulting interval is often a quicker means of recognizing larger, more complex intervals.

Example 10.20
Using inversion to determine interval size

Identifying Compound Intervals

Compound intervals are first recognized as being larger than an octave. To help recognize and identify them correctly, it is helpful to first reduce them to within one octave of each other, then to identify the simple interval, and finally to add seven to the general interval number for the first octave and eight for each additional octave, keeping the same specific **quality** as the reduced, simple interval you previously determined.

Example 10.21
Identifying compound intervals

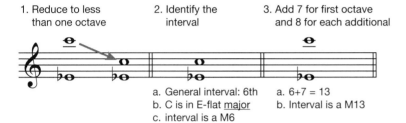

1. Reduce to less than one octave
2. Identify the interval
3. Add 7 for first octave and 8 for each additional

a. General interval: 6th
b. C is in E-flat major
c. interval is a M6

a. 6+7 = 13
b. Interval is a M13

10.9 Writing Intervals

Intervals Above a Given Pitch

When asked to write an ascending **melodic** or **harmonic** interval above a given note, all of the previous methods may be used to determine the correct pitch. As long as the following steps are strictly adhered to, all will result in the correct interval:

1. Notate the starting pitch (if not given).

2. Notate the general interval of the requested interval above the given pitch.

3. Chromatically alter the upper note (if needed) to form the requested interval using whatever method is easiest for you (chromatic counting, scale recognition, relating to a known interval, using inversion, etc.).

For example: notate the pitch an augmented sixth above F4.

Example 10.22
Writing ascending intervals

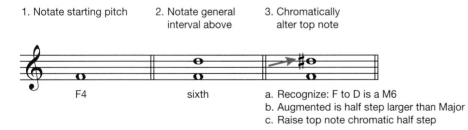

1. Notate starting pitch
2. Notate general interval above
3. Chromatically alter top note

F4

sixth

a. Recognize: F to D is a M6
b. Augmented is half step larger than Major
c. Raise top note chromatic half step

Intervals Below a Given Pitch

When asked to write a descending melodic or harmonic interval below a given note, not all of the previous methods may be as useful. Since the lower note is not yet known, it cannot be used to determine if the upper note is in the scale of that note. For this reason, **chromatic counting** for smaller intervals (seconds, thirds, and fourths) and use of **inversions** for larger intervals (fifths, sixths, and sevenths) are often the fastest and most accurate methods for writing these intervals. Of course, if after step 2 the pitch is recognized as the correct interval, you are done. The following steps, similar to those for ascending intervals, will help to prevent errors:

1. Notate the starting pitch (if not given).

2. Notate the general interval of the requested interval below the given pitch.

3. Chromatically alter the lower note (if needed) to form the requested interval using whatever method is easiest for you (chromatic counting, relating to a known interval, using inversion, etc.).

Example: notate the pitch a major seventh below D5.

Example 10.23
Writing descending intervals

1. Notate starting pitch   2. Notate general   3. Chromatically
                               interval below   alter lower note

D5   seventh   a. Know: M7 inverts to a m2
                                                     b. E-flat is a m2 above D
                                                     c. E-flat below is a M7

Writing Compound Intervals

For **compound intervals**, either ascending or descending, first determine the simple interval to which it reduces using the previous procedures and then add additional octaves to the new second note to form the requested interval.

As with all intervals, it is important not to change the starting, given pitch, only the second, requested pitch. Although this may seem obvious, it is one of the more common errors.

In the chapters ahead, the principle of intervallic inversion will become quite important in understanding the use of **chords** and melodic function. For this reason, a thorough mastery of identifying and writing intervals and their inversions is essential before moving ahead.

Chapter Summary

An **interval** is the distance between any two pitches. **Melodic intervals** are found between any two notes occurring separately, one after the other. **Harmonic intervals** occur simultaneously. Both are measured using the same principles.

General intervals measure the distance based upon the number of **scale degrees** separating the two pitches, and is used to understand general relationships between notes. **Specific intervals** measure the distance between two notes exactly, and are notated using the general interval number and the interval's **quality**. Specific interval qualities are normally either **perfect** (P), **major** (M), **minor** (m), **diminished** (dim or °), or **augmented** (Aug or +). Rarely one finds intervals that are **doubly diminished** or **doubly augmented**. The perfect intervals are unisons, fourths, fifths, and the octave when their half step content is 0, 5, 7, and 12, respectively. The other general intervals within the octave, **seconds**, **thirds**, **sixths**, and **sevenths** may be either major or minor depending on their half-step content. All perfect and minor intervals become diminished when reduced by a chromatic half step, and all perfect and major intervals become augmented when enlarged by a chromatic half step.

Compound intervals are those greater than an octave, and are commonly notated only up to a thirteenth. Compound intervals are also frequently **reduced** to their simple counterparts via **octave equivalence**.

All intervals may be **inverted** by **transposing** the lower note by a perfect octave to be above the upper note, or vice versa. Inverted intervals exhibit a mirror relationship around the interval of a **tritone**.

A variety of techniques for quickly recognizing and writing intervals are available, including use of major and minor scales, comparison to a known, close interval, and chromatic counting, and it is essential for musicians to be able to visually and aurally recognize them all before more advanced study and music making can begin.

Aural Drill: Diatonic Intervals

1   Sing using your chosen sight singing syllables:

a) **Major**

b) **Minor**

2 Sing the following using your chosen sight singing syllables for the first two beats of each measure, then use the interval name for the last two beats as given:

a) Major

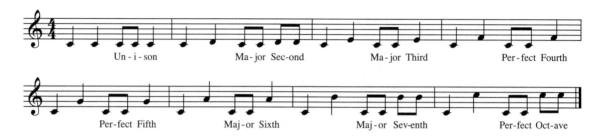

b) Minor

Chapter 10 Exercises

1 Identify the general interval number for each of the following melodic intervals
(as per Table 10.1), then notate each as a harmonic interval above the lowest
note:

_____   _____   _____   _____   _____   _____

2 Label the general interval between each note of the following melody (Vivaldi:
"Spring" from *The Four Seasons*, Mvt. 2 mm. 8–15) and identify the key it is in:

Key: _____

3 Write the specified general melodic interval:

a) up a 5th   **b)** down a 3rd **c)** up a 7th   **d)** up a 4th   **e)** up a 2nd   **f)** down a 6th

g) up a 6th   **h)** down a 5th **i)** up a 4th   **j)** down a 2nd **k)** unison   **l)** up an octave

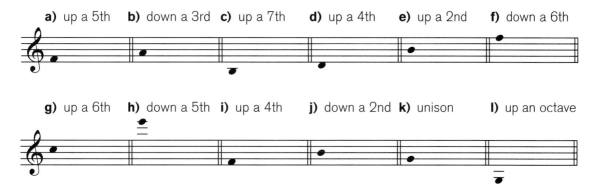

4 Specify the general interval (G.I.), number of half steps (½) between the two
pitches, and the specific interval (S.I.) as requested:

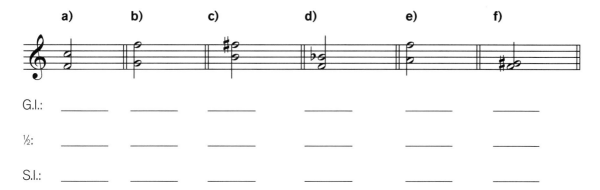

G.I.: _____   _____   _____   _____   _____   _____

½: _____   _____   _____   _____   _____   _____

S.I.: _____   _____   _____   _____   _____   _____

G.I.: _____   _____   _____   _____   _____   _____

½: _____   _____   _____   _____   _____   _____

S.I.: _____   _____   _____   _____   _____   _____

5   Identify the specific interval as given, then add an accidental to the second note of
each to form the requested interval:

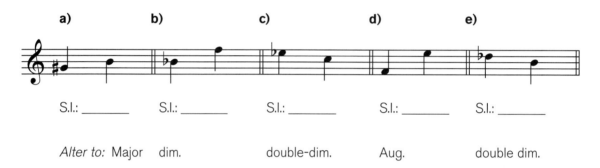

S.I.: _____   S.I.: _____   S.I.: _____   S.I.: _____   S.I.: _____

Alter to: Major   dim.   double-dim.   Aug.   double dim.

6   Reduce the following compound intervals to their simple counterparts
(as a harmonic interval) then identify both specific intervals:

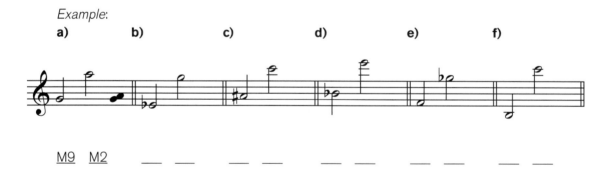

<u>M9</u> <u>M2</u>   __ __   __ __   __ __   __ __   __ __

7   Specify the interval quality into which each given quality inverts:

a)   M invert into: _____

b)   m inverts into: _____

c)   + inverts into: _____

d)   P inverts into: _____

8 Identify the given interval, then identify and write the inversion, using the first note of the original:

Example:

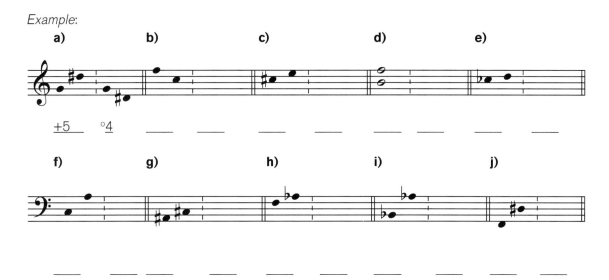

a) +5   °4

b) ____   ____

c) ____   ____

d) ____   ____

e) ____   ____

f) ____   ____

g) ____   ____

h) ____   ____

i) ____   ____

j) ____   ____

9 Write the intervals as either melodic (mel) or harmonic (har) as requested:

a) mel — up P5
b) mel — up m7
c) har — down P4
d) mel — down M9
e) mel — down m6
f) har — up +8

g) har — up P4
h) mel — down m3
i) har — up m2
j) mel — up P11
k) mel — down °7
l) mel — up +3

m) mel — up P5
n) har — down °2
o) mel — down +5
p) har — down M7
q) mel — down M9
r) har — down tritone

s) har — up M3
t) mel — up M6
u) har — up +2
v) mel — down m6
w) har — up M7
x) mel — up P8

Triads and Seventh Chords

11.1 Triads

A **chord** is a collection of three or more pitch classes that sound together (when only two pitch classes sound together, it is simply an **interval**). Chords in the **tonal** system are based on the three most stable pitch classes of the **overtone series**, which is the acoustic basis for musical sound and our tonal system of music. The overtone series is a series of pitches created by multiples of the **frequency** of the lowest pitch (x). The first six notes of the overtone series built upon the pitch C2 are shown in Example 11.1. (For more information on the overtone series, see **Appendix 2**.) Notice that when these first six notes of the overtone series are reduced to within an octave, the **pitch classes** are each a **third** apart and correspond to scale degrees 1, 3, and 5 in the major scale using the lowest note as tonic. **Tonal harmony** is based upon this principle of chords containing stacked thirds. This is also referred to as **functional tertian harmony**. This most common form of three notes that can be arranged in stacked thirds is called a **triad**.

Example 11.1
Deriving triads from the overtone series

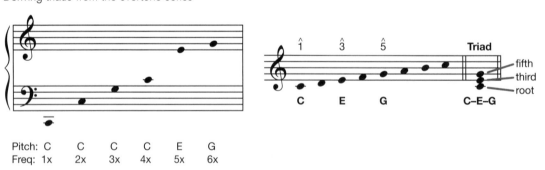

Pitch:	C	C	C	C	E	G
Freq:	1x	2x	3x	4x	5x	6x

The lowest pitch class of a triad in this basic arrangement of stacked thirds (Example 11.1) is called the **root**. The names of other notes of the triad are derived from their **general intervals** above the root: the **third** and the **fifth**. Typically, when referring to triads in general, this tightly spaced arrangement above the root is used, and it is referred to as **root position**. The triad is spelled from the root up (i.e. in the above example: C-E-G).

In tonal music, a root position, **diatonic** triad may be built on any scale degree by adding a third and a fifth from the same scale above it:

Example 11.2
Triads on each scale degree

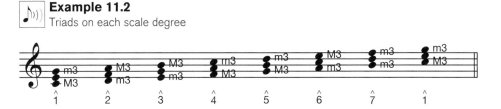

Notice that although the **triads** all consist of stacked major and/or minor thirds, they may occur in different combinations and result in different sounds. The **quality** of a triad depends how the minor and/or major thirds are arranged. In major keys, triads built on scale degrees 1, 4, and 5 consist of a M3 on the bottom and a m3 on the top. We call this a **major triad**. The triads built on scale degrees 2, 3, and 6 consist of a m3 on the bottom and a M3 on the top. We call this a **minor triad**. Both are considered **stable** chords because of the very stable P5 interval formed between the root and the fifth by the combination of the two thirds (see **Appendix 2** for a more detailed discussion of **consonance** and **dissonance**).

Example 11.3
Major and minor triad construction

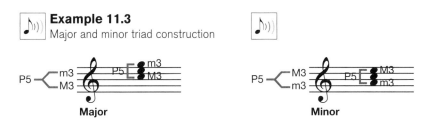

The triad build on scale degree 7 is different. It consists of two minor thirds that result in an unstable, dissonant, diminished fifth between the root and the fifth when combined. Because of the quality of the fifth, this type of triad is called a **diminished triad**. A fourth and more rare type of triad results when two major thirds are combined, resulting in an augmented fifth. This type of triad is referred to as an **augmented triad**. Because both the diminished and augmented triads contain the unstable intervals of a diminished fifth or an augmented fifth, these are considered less stable chords than major or minor triads.

Example 11.4
Diminished and augmented triads

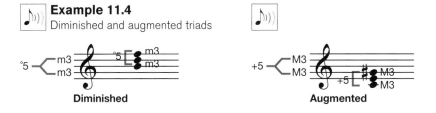

In all there are four possible triad qualities: **major**, **minor**, **diminished**, and **augmented**. Triads containing augmented or diminished thirds rarely occur in tonal music, so they do not have common names. Triads are identified by the letter name of their **root** and the triad **quality**, as in C major or B diminished.

11.2 Seventh Chords

By adding another third on top of a triad, we create a more dissonant chord because it includes the interval of a seventh. This type of chord is called a **seventh chord**. Like triads, the names of the notes of the seventh are derived from their interval above the **root**: the **third**, the **fifth**, and the **seventh**.

Example 11.5
Seventh chord construction

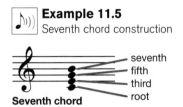

Since four pitch classes are present, there are more combinations of stacks of major and minor thirds possible. In tonal music, however, only certain combinations are commonly used. Seventh chords built upon augmented triads are extremely rare, as are minor triads with a major seventh and major or minor triads with diminished sevenths. There are five seventh chord qualities that were commonly used in the common-practice period. These are listed in Table 11.1.

Table 11.1 Seventh chords

Description	Abbreviation	Construction	Audio example
Major-Major 7th	MM7	M + M7 = MM7	
Major-minor 7th (Dominant 7th)	Mm7	M + m7 = Mm7	
Minor-minor 7th	mm7	m + m7 = mm7	
Half-diminished 7th	ø7	° + m7 = ø7	
Fully diminished 7th	°7	° + °7 = °7	

11.3 Pop/Jazz Chord Symbols

There are several common ways to refer to various **chords**. The most general method is used in popular and jazz music and involves referring to the pitch class that serves as the **root** of the chord. Alterations to the basic chord or added tones such as sevenths are

Table 11.2 Pop/jazz chord symbols

Description	Pop/jazz symbol	Construction	Audio example
Major triad	C		
Minor triad	Am		
Augmented triad	C+		
Diminished triad	Bdim		
Major-Major 7th	Cmaj7	M + M7 = MM7	
Major-minor 7th (Dominant 7th)	C7	M + m7 = Mm7	
Minor-Minor 7th	Cm7	m + mM7 = mm7	
Half-diminished 7th	Cm7♭5	° + m7 = °7	
Fully diminished 7th	o7	° + °7 = °7	

notated with additional symbols. This system of notating chords does not specify how the chord functions or relates to other chords, but is a very simple and easy way of specifying the spelling and quality of the chord. Table 11.2 lists these symbols.

11.4 Roman Numerals

In common practice music, there is a different method of specifying chords that reflects their relationships to a particular key. This method uses **Roman numerals** to indicate the **scale degree** upon which the chord is built instead of pitch names. In most schools in the United States, the Roman numeral is upper case for major chords, upper case with a superscripted "+" for **augmented** chords, lower case for minor, and lower case plus a superscript "o" (°) for **diminished** triads. This method uses a superscripted "M7" (^{M7})to indicate a chord with a major seventh, a superscripted "7" (^{7}) to indicate chords with a minor seventh, a superscripted "ø" (^{ø}) for **half diminished seventh chords** (diminished chords with a minor seventh), and a superscripted "o" (°) for **fully diminished seventh chords** (a diminished chord with a diminished seventh). The case of the Roman numeral is used to determine whether the triad within the seventh chord is major or minor (i.e. an upper case Roman numeral with a "7" (V^{7}) is a major triad with a minor seventh, a lower case Roman numeral with a "7" (v^{7}) is a minor triad with a minor seventh). Augmented chords do not have functional sevenths added to them, so there is no standard symbol for them. Example 11.6 lists the most common chords and their Roman numeral symbols for major and minor keys. It also lists other possible chords formed by the melodic minor scale. These less common chords will be found in compositions, but far more rarely than the first set.

Example 11.6
Triads and seventh chords in major and minor keys

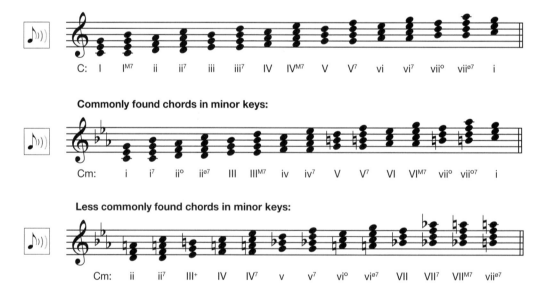

Using Roman numerals alone allows for the discussion of the general functions of tonal harmonies. Although this example is in C, the same chord qualities, *and therefore the same Roman numerals*, would be used for the chords built on the same scale degrees for *all* major or minor keys using the same forms of the minor scale. In major keys, the chord built on scale degree 1 is always a **I** chord, on scale degree 2 is always a **ii** chord, and so forth as noted in Example 11.6. This is one of the strengths of this method of specifying chords: no matter what the key, the chord built on each scale degree functions in the same manner, has the same quality, and uses the same symbol. Chromatic raising or lowering of a pitch, as used in the minor chords in this example, always change the chords in the same way and result in the same new Roman numerals that function in the same way. It is this consistency of function that makes this method of referring to chords the preferred choice for most music theory studies, and will be the method used in this text.

You will find some texts based on the nineteenth-century approach use all upper case Roman numerals and omit symbols that specify the chord quality. In that system, the key must always be specified and the accidentals in the key signature must be considered in order to determine the chord quality. Other texts may use both upper and lower case Roman numerals and all of the symbols except the M7 for chords containing major sevenths. If your instructor is using one of these texts for future music theory courses, he or she may ask you to ignore the "M" and simply use a "7" for chords containing either diatonic major or minor sevenths.

11.5 Reduction of Chords

When asked to write chords from a given Roman numeral, they are generally written in **root position** in the most tightly spaced arrangement, as shown in the examples to this point in the chapter. However, in actual music, chords may be constructed in a wide variety of arrangements. In musical passages it is common for one or more of the pitches in a **triad**, most often the **root**, to be duplicated in another octave or as a unison. For the purposes of identifying a Roman numeral, duplication of a pitch in the chord will have no effect on the identity of the Roman numeral due to the principle of **octave equivalence**. In addition, the identity of the Roman numeral will not be affected by the arrangement of pitches above the lowest note of the chord. In Example 11.7, the chords in each example use the same pitch classes, but only differ in the arrangement of the notes in different octaves above the lowest note. As long as the lowest note and **pitch classes** used remain the same, the same Roman numeral is used to identify these chords.

Example 11.7
Reduction of chords in open spacing

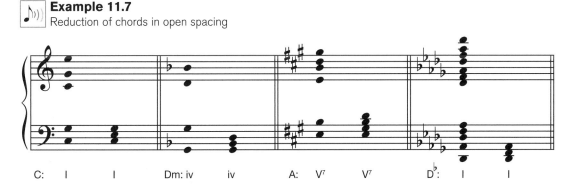

When asked to identify chords, the notes may be in any octave arrangement above the lowest note, often referred to as the **bass**. This can sometimes make it difficult to identify the chord. By reducing the chord to the tightest arrangement of pitches above the bass and removing all duplicates, identification of the chord is much easier, as demonstrated in Example 11.8.

Example 11.8
Reductions of chords for analysis

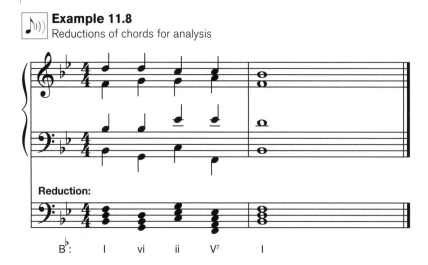

B♭: I   vi   ii   V⁷   I

Whenever reducing chords, it is vital that the notes never be notated below the given **bass note**. In tonal music, the bass note has a powerful function. Changing which pitch is in the lowest position changes the function of the chord, as will be discussed in the next chapter.

Chapter Summary

A **chord** is a collection of three or more notes. **Tonal harmony** is based upon the principle of chords composed of pitch classes that are each a **third** apart, as derived from the **overtone series**. A three-note chord in stacked thirds is called a **triad**. The lowest note of a triad is called the **root**. The upper two notes derive their names from their **interval** above the root: the middle note is called the **third**, and the top note is called the **fifth** of the chord. Triads have four basic types: **major** (M3+m3, from the root up), **minor** (m3+M3), **Augmented** (M3+M3), and **diminished** (m3+m3). They are abbreviated, respectively, as: M, m, +, °.

A **seventh chord** adds a fourth note to the triad: a **seventh** above the root. They are commonly found in the following forms: **Major-Major seventh chords**, **Major-minor seventh chords**, **minor-minor seventh chords**, **half-diminished seventh chords**, and **fully diminished seventh chords**. They are abbreviated, respectively, as: MM7, Mm7, mm7, ø7, °7.

Chords with the root as the lowest note are said to be in **root position**.

Pop (or Jazz) chord symbols label chords according to the pitch class of the root, plus various symbols to specify which notes are found above the root (i.e. Cmaj7).

Roman numeral analysis is a traditional method of labeling chords according to their function, and uses Roman numerals corresponding to the **scale degree** of the **root** of the chord. In the United States, major chords use upper case Roman numerals, minor chords use lower case, **augmented** chords use upper case with a superscript "+", and **diminished** chords use lower case with a superscript "o." Seventh chords add a "M7" for major seventh chords, a "7" for minor seventh chords, a "ø7" for half-diminished seventh chords, and a "°7" for fully diminished seventh chords, all in superscript following the appropriate Roman numeral. Because Roman numerals reflect the chord **quality** and function defined by the scale degree upon which they are built, they are used in this text, and for most music theory courses, to discuss and analyze tonal music in all major or minor keys.

Through the principle of **octave equivalence**, chords can be **reduced** to within one octave above the bass and duplicate pitches can be removed without changing the chord's identity or function. This greatly simplifies the identification of chords. In doing so, however, one must not **transpose** any pitch below the bass, as in tonal music this changes the function of the chord.

Aural Drill: Diatonic Triads

1   Sing the following with the recorded block chord accompaniment using your chosen sight singing syllables:

a) **Major** 🎵

b) **Minor** 🎵

Chapter 11 Exercises

1 Add the qualities (P, M, m, +, °) to the given general intervals to specify the specific interval qualities of the four triad types (as in Examples 11.3 and 11.4):

a) Major **b)** Minor **c)** Augmented **d)** Diminished

P5 ⎰ __3 / __3   __5 ⎰ __3 / __3   __5 ⎰ __3 / __3   __5 ⎰ __3 / __3

2 Summarize the stacks of thirds in each chord, as above using M or m. Memorize these stacks:

a) Augmented **b)** Minor **c)** Diminished **d)** Major

Example: M

  M   ____   ____   ____

3 Given the root and quality, spell the triads:

Example: C maj: CEG

a) D dim: ___ ___ ___   **b)** G min: ___ ___ ___

c) F aug: ___ ___ ___   **d)** E maj: ___ ___ ___

e) B-flat dim: ___ ___ ___ **f)** F-sharp maj: ___ ___ ___

g) C-sharp dim: ___ ___ ___ **h)** A aug: ___ ___ ___

i) G-flat dim: ___ ___ ___

4 Add the interval qualities (M, m, °) to the general intervals provided for each of the seventh chord types to specify the quality of the seventh and of each third in the stack, then memorize.

Example:

a) MM7 **b)** Mm7 **c)** mm7

M 7 ⎰ M 3 / m 3 / M 3   __7 ⎰ __3 / __3 / __3   __7 ⎰ __3 / __3 / __3

d) °7 **e)** °7.

__7 ⎰ __3 / __3 / __3   __7 ⎰ __3 / __3 / __3

5 Given the root and quality, spell the seventh chords, as in number 3 opposite:

a) C Mm7: ___ ___ ___ ___   **b)** D-sharp °7: ___ ___ ___ ___

c) G mm7: ___ ___ ___ ___   **d)** E-flat MM7: ___ ___ ___ ___

e) B-flat °7: ___ ___ ___ ___   **f)** E ⌀7: ___ ___ ___ ___

g) F-sharp °7: ___ ___ ___ ___   **h)** A-flat Mm7: ___ ___ ___ ___

6 Identify each chord using the appropriate pop/jazz chord symbol:

a) _____   **b)** _____   **c)** _____   **d)** _____   **e)** _____   **f)** _____

7 Notate the chords indicated by the pop symbols in root position. Be sure to add accidentals if the chord has pitches that are *not* in the given key signature:

a) B7   **b)** E7   **c)** Amaj7   **d)** D   **e)** D#m7♭5   **f)** EMaj7

8 Renotate the incorrect given chord to match the pop/jazz chord symbol:

a) F7   **b)** F#dim7   **c)** G7   **d)** d#dim7   **e)** Bm

9 Identify the *key* and the Roman numeral for the given chords. The first is completed for you. Minor keys may contain less common variants:

Major Keys

a) E♭: vi   **b)** ___ : ___   **c)** ___ : ___   **d)** ___ : ___   **e)** ___ : ___

f) ___ : ___   **g)** ___ : ___   **h)** ___ : ___   **i)** ___ : ___   **j)** ___ : ___

Minor Keys

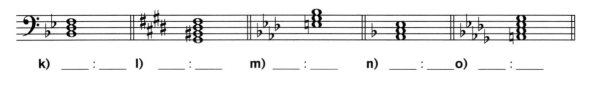

k) ____ : ____   l) ____ : ____   m) ____ : ____   n) ____ : ____   o) ____ : ____

p) ____ : ____   q) ____ : ____   r) ____ : ____   s) ____ : ____   t) ____ : ____

10 Write the requested *key signature* and *chord* in close spacing, root position:

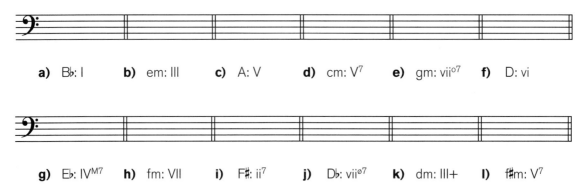

a) B♭: I   **b)** em: III   **c)** A: V   **d)** cm: V⁷   **e)** gm: vii°⁷   **f)** D: vi

g) E♭: IVᴹ⁷   **h)** fm: VII   **i)** F♯: ii⁷   **j)** D♭: vii°⁷   **k)** dm: III+   **l)** f♯m: V⁷

11 For each chord create a reduction above the bass note and provide the requested information below. The first is completed as an example:

D Major:

Root: D   ____ ____ ____ ____   ____ ____ ____ ____

Quality: M   ____ ____ ____ ____   ____ ____ ____ ____

Roman
Numeral: I   ____ ____ ____ ____   ____ ____ ____ ____

Pop/Jazz: D   ____ ____ ____ ____   ____ ____ ____ ____

CHAPTER 12

Inversion of Chords and Figured Bass

12.1 Inversion of Chords

All of the chords in the **previous chapter** were in **root position**, which means that they all have the **root** of the **chord** as the lowest note. This is the most stable form for a chord, since pitch classes of the chord most strongly re-enforce the **overtone series** of the **bass note**. However, if another member of the chord, such as the **third**, is in the bass, the other chord tones will not match the lower **overtone series** for that pitch, and the chord will not be as stable. When a pitch class other than the root of the chord is in the bass, it is said that the chord is **inverted**. When the third of the chord is the lowest pitch, the chord is in **first inversion**. When the **fifth** of the chord is in the bass, it is in **second inversion**. If the **seventh** of a chord is the lowest pitch, the chord is in **third inversion**.

Example 12.1
Inversion of triads and seventh chords

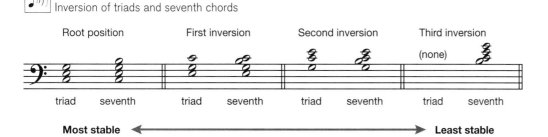

As chords are inverted farther from root position, they become less and less stable. Composers use this instability to create a sense of forward motion in music as unstable chords move forward into more stable chords. As our common practice tonal system was being developed, composers recognized the importance of the bass note and inversions and they were very specific in their notation of these two important traits. This, then, developed into our modern day method of notating inversions.

12.2 Figured Bass

In the **Baroque** period (*c.*1600–*c.*1750), composers frequently wrote music using a type of musical shorthand called **figured bass**. Figured bass notation consists of a bass note with small numbers and/or accidentals below the bass note called **figured bass symbols**, which indicate the intervals of the pitches above that note. This simple notation is called the **basso continuo** part. The bass line was played by a instrument such as a bassoon, a low string instrument similar to our modern 'cello, or whatever similar instrument was available, and by a keyboard player (organ, harpsichord, clavichord, or whatever was available) who would also play the bass line in the left hand and use the figured bass symbols to determine the chord to be played in the right hand. This chord could be a simple **block chord** or an improvised passage based on that chord depending on the style of the piece. This procedure is similar to the way that jazz and rock musicians use Pop/Jazz chord symbols today. This improvised performance of the figured bass, when written out, is called a **realization**, which includes the chords specified by the figured bass along with optional **embellishments** such as trills (*tr*) and grace notes (smaller notes). One possible realization is shown in Example 12.2.

Example 12.2
Figured bass notation in the basso continuo part and realization

A root position triad, such as the second chord in Example 12.2, has a third (3) and a fifth (5) above the bass note, so its full figured bass symbol would be a 5 above a 3. However, since root position chords are so common, composers began to omit these numbers and assume the performers would recognize an unmarked bass note as a root position triad above that note. Similarly, in other common chords, composers used the least amount of figured bass numbers to specify the correct chords. This saved time in writing the music and simplified the amount of information the performers needed to realize the figured bass. For **seventh chords**, figured bass can be reduced to only as few as two numbers to show what inversion the chord is in, and the most common number, usually a 3 or a 6, is often omitted. Table 12.1 lists all of the figured bass symbols for all inversions.

In addition to the numbers listed in Table 12.1, other numbers such as 4, 9, and 2 may appear in figured bass. These were added to specify notes at that **general interval** above the **bass** that are not part of the chords, but still function in a linear manner and therefore were necessary to specify (i.e. a 4 indicates a **fourth** above the bass note that normally resolves down to a **third**, just like the **tendency tone** of scale degree 4 resolving down to 3 in major keys).

An accidental before a number indicates that the same accidental should be added to the corresponding note which is that **general interval** above the bass (i.e. a sharp in front of a 6 means that the note a sixth above the bass should have a sharp added). This works the same way no matter what the accidental: sharp, flat or natural. An accidental without

Table 12.1 Figured bass symbols

Inversion and chord type	Full figured bass symbol	Common figured bass symbol	Close spacing realization (above "C")	Audio example
Root position triad	5 3	(nothing)		🔊
First inversion triad	6 3	6		🔊
Second inversion triad	6 4	6 4		🔊
Root position seventh chord	7 5 3	7		🔊
First inversion seventh chord	6 5 3	6 5		🔊
Second inversion seventh chord	6 4 3	4 3		🔊
Third inversion seventh chord	6 4 2	4 2		🔊

a number indicates that the third above the bass is to have that accidental applied (the "3" is omitted because this is such a common alteration). The most common **chromatic alteration** occurs in minor keys, when scale degrees 6 and/or 7 are raised a chromatic half step to fit the **melodic** or **harmonic** minor scales. Since these were so common, composers used a **backslash** through a number to indicate that the corresponding pitch that interval above the bass was to be raised one chromatic half step. If it was a flat in the key signature, it becomes a natural; if it was a natural, it becomes a sharp, etc.

Sometimes the bass line would function as a short melodic passage, and a line under it would indicate that the same chord played at the beginning should continue through that passage without changing to a new chord on each bass note.

The octave arrangement of the notes above the bass note is the only thing not specified by the **inversion symbols** and **figured bass**. It makes no difference at all how the pitches are vertically arranged in this style, as long as all the correct pitch classes are present and certain stylistic principles are observed. However, a skilled performer would create interesting, musical, and often quite virtuosic realizations that fit the melodic and rhythmic motives that the composer had written.

Example 12.3 contains examples of all of these alterations in a simple **realization**, shown below the flute and **basso continuo** parts.

Example 12.3

Figured bass notation and realization: Handel, Sonata VII for Flute and Basso Continuo, Mvt. II, mm. 11–14

These **figured bass symbols** are the basis for the **inversion symbols** in use today with **Roman numerals**. Besides forming a background for better understanding our modern system, figured bass realization allows for the performance of a vast amount of music from the Baroque period, much of which does not have a published, written-out realization available.

12.3 Roman Numeral Analysis with Inversion Symbols

Our modern **inversion symbols** are only slightly different from figured bass. These inversion symbols, when combined with a **Roman numeral**/chord **quality** symbol (i.e. IV^M7) and a key signature, fully identify the pitch classes present in the chord and which note is in the bass. The important difference between the **figured bass symbols** in Table 12.1 and the inversion symbols in Table 12.2 is that **figured bass** is always attached to a specific bass note, and uses accidentals to indicate the actual pitch classes and chord quality. Inversion symbols are always attached to a **Roman numeral** which specifies the functional **root** and **quality** for any key. Only when a key is specified are actual pitches specified.

Table 12.2 lists all inversions of triads and seventh chords and shows both their full figured bass and inversion symbols. These are an essential part of analyzing and labeling chords, and both the inversion numbers and the visual identification on the staff of the pitches in block chords should be memorized.

Triads only have two symbols: a 6 for first inversion triads and a 6 over 4 for second inversion triads. A helpful way to memorize the inversion numbers for seventh chords is that they count backwards from 7 (just like creating the **key signature tools**) with the 4 duplicating: 7, 6–5, 4–3, 4–2.

When analyzing music, one of the first steps is to reduce the music to a **block chord** above the bass, as demonstrated in the **previous chapter**. Once this is done, the chord will most often look like one of the illustrations in Table 12.2. There is a very simple and fast way to identify both the root and the inversion of a chord once it is in this block arrangement above the bass:

Table 12.2 Inversion symbols

Inversion and chord type	Full figured bass symbol	Inversion symbol following a Roman numeral	Close spacing example	Audio example
Root position triad	5 3	(nothing)	A: I	
First inversion triad	6 3	6	A: I^6	
Second inversion triad	6 4	6 4	A: I$^6_4$	
Root position seventh chord	7 5 3	7	A: I^{M7}	
First inversion seventh chord	6 5 3	6 5	A: I$^{M6}_5$	
Second inversion seventh chord	6 4 3	4 3	A: I$^{M4}_3$	
Third inversion seventh chord	6 4 2	4 2	A: I$^{M4}_2$	

- First, identify the interval that is *not a third* (it will be either a fourth for triads, or a second for seventh chords).

- The *top* note of that interval is the root of that chord (the pitch "A" in the examples in Table 12.2).

- The number of notes *above* the interval that is not a third indicates the inversion:

  - one note above the not-a-third interval indicates first inversion

  - two notes above the not-a-third indicates second inversion

  - three notes above the not-a-third indicates third inversion

  - all thirds (zero "not-a-thirds") is root position.

Once the root and the key signature are known, the correct **Roman numeral** and chord **quality** can be determined. When the correct **inversion symbol** is added to this Roman numeral symbol, the result is a complete method of specifying a **harmony** that allows you to identify and hear relationships. Notice how the two excerpts in Example 12.4 sound related, although they are in different keys and look rather different in their notation. A Roman numeral analysis of each shows the reason for this similarity: they both have identical **harmonic** content.

Example 12.4
Two musical passages with the same harmonic structure

Labeling the chords is only the first step. After labeling these chords, the **harmonic function** may be examined. This is the focus of Music Theory. However, before any analysis of function can begin, a student must thoroughly master identifying the fundamental components of music.

Chapter Summary

Root position chords are the most stable since the notes of the chord re-inforce the **overtone series**. When a chord tone other than the **root** is in the **bass**, the chord is **inverted**. **First inversion chords** have the **third** of the chord in the bass, **second inversion chords** have the **fifth** in the bass, and for seventh chords, **third inversion chords** have the **seventh** in the bass. As chords invert farther from root position, they become less stable—a trait composers use to create harmonic motion in their works.

Figured bass is a form of notation used in the Baroque period that specifies **harmonies** in a **basso continuo** part, consisting of a **bass line** (notated) plus **figured bass symbols**. These symbols indicate the **general intervals** above the bass note of the other notes in the chord, and are often abbreviated to use the minimum number of symbols to specify the desired harmony. To save time in both reading and writing figured bass, composers omitted the 5 and 3 in root position chords, the 3 in first inversion chords, and the 6 in second and third inversion seventh chords. **Accidentals** added before a number are applied to the corresponding note for that **general interval** above the bass. A **backslash** through a number means to raise that corresponding note by a **chromatic half step**. Other numbers such as 4, 8, and 9 were added to specify linear and melodic tones.

Performers **improvise** the notes specified by the figured bass in real-time. A **realization** is a written-out version of the figured bass.

Modern-day **inversion symbols** are based on figured bass notation. The following lists these symbols:

	Triads	Seventh chords
Root position:	(none)	7
First inversion:	6	$\frac{6}{5}$
Second inversion:	$\frac{6}{4}$	$\frac{4}{3}$
Third inversion	—	$\frac{4}{2}$

When added to a Roman numeral symbol instead of under a notated bass note, the result is a **Roman numeral analysis** that identifies and specifies the **quality**, **function**, and **inversion** of a **chord**. This allows for the analysis of **tonal** music and can be used to identify relationships that remain the same for music in any key.

Aural Drill: Inversion of Major and Minor Triads

1   Sing using your chosen sight singing syllables with the recorded block chords:

a) **Major** 🎵))

b) **Minor** 🎵))

Chapter 12 Exercises

1 If the chord is not in root position (all thirds) draw a line between the two notes
that are not a third apart. Next, determine the root, fill in that notehead, and write its
pitch class below. Finally, label the inversion (root, 1st, 2nd, or 3rd) and the correct
inversion symbol (I.S.) from Table 12.2:

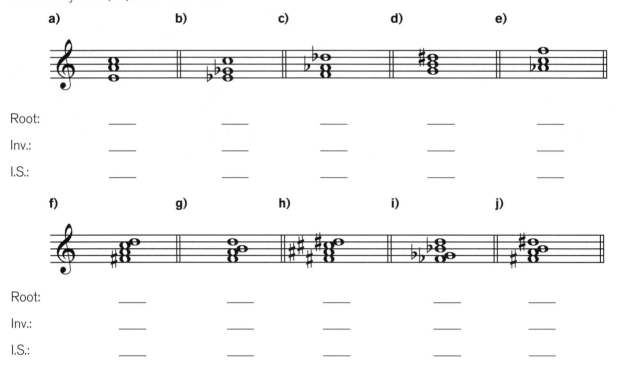

Root: ____ ____ ____ ____ ____

Inv.: ____ ____ ____ ____ ____

I.S.: ____ ____ ____ ____ ____

Root: ____ ____ ____ ____ ____

Inv.: ____ ____ ____ ____ ____

I.S.: ____ ____ ____ ____ ____

2 Realize the figured bass in block chords in the staff above. You may add optional
embellishments if you wish, but should not change the chord itself:

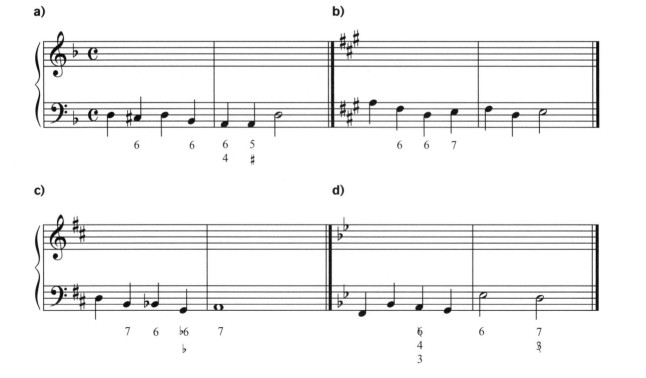

3 Notate the chords specified by the figured bass in block chords in the middle staff. Then add the appropriate root and Roman numeral (R.N.) for that chord below. Remember that the half note in measure 2 continues to the end of the measure. The CD-ROM has a recording of this example:

Handel, Sonata in A Minor for flute and basso continuo HWV. 374, IV, mm 1–3

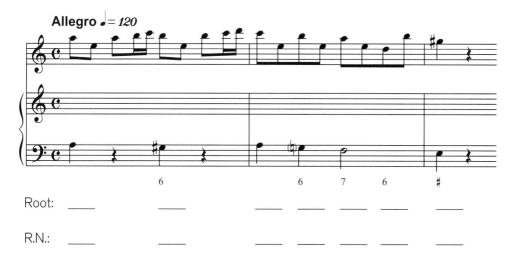

Root: ____   ____   ____ ____ ____ ____   ____

R.N.: ____   ____   ____ ____ ____ ____   ____

4 Provide the key and a Roman numeral analysis, including inversion symbols, below each chord. The CD-ROM has a recording of these examples:

a) Major

Key ____: ____ ____ ____ ____   ____ ____ ____ ____   ____

b) Minor

Key ___: ____ ____ ____ ____   ____ ____ ____ ____   ____ ____ ____

CHAPTER 13

Application to Analysis: Chords and Melody in Musical Practice

Up to this point, the examples have been isolated and brief to allow for the identification and demonstration of various elements of music. In musical practice, however, all of these elements are used together to form an artistic whole, and this may seem at first a bit overwhelming. **Musical analysis** is a process that takes complex music and focuses on one aspect at a time, breaking it down into simpler, more understandable units, then identifies and labels these elements and their relationships so that a deeper understanding of the music is possible. As a result, performers are able to make better performance decisions and give more expressive and stylistically correct performances. Listeners are able to hear and appreciate music at a deeper level. Composers are able to understand the techniques used by others and incorporate those into their own works. Musical analysis forms the basis of advanced music studies. The scope of this text is to provide a thorough and solid foundation in recognizing and labeling these fundamental musical elements so that aspiring musicians are able to move ahead into these more advanced studies. This chapter concludes with a brief introduction to the first step in musical analysis: the identification of the basic elements studied to this point. This also serves as a synthesis and review of these materials in a practical, direct application to real music. As you study these elements, see if you recognize them in the music you are playing, bring these to your instructor, and share your findings. Your instructor may also have other pieces to study. Remember: these fundamentals are most easily recognized and found in music of the earlier common practice period, and more advanced examples will no doubt be explained in future music theory courses.

13.1 Musical Texture and Harmonic Analysis

In musical practice, **chords** may appear in their simple, tightly spaced form, but more often the notes of the chord are arranged in a wide variety of manners, depending on the style and effect the composer intends. **Texture** in music refers to how many **voices** (the consistent number of notes in the chord or single-note parts sounding at once, whether instrumental, keyboard, or vocal) there are in a passage of music and how the voices are arranged and relate to each other. As far as the number of voices typically used in the common practice period, although there may be many instruments or voices sounding at once, most pieces can be reduced to three or four part textures. The standard number of voices in choral music, for example, is four: the soprano, alto, tenor, and bass (**SATB**). Based upon the strong choral tradition, four-part **harmony** was the standard approach for much of the common practice period, and for this reason it is used for many harmonic examples in music theory. As for how these voices relate to each other, there are three basic textures that describe most of the music of the common practice period: **monophonic**, **homophonic**, and **polyphonic**. Each of these terms is discussed below. Since it is easy to identify chords in a homophonic texture, it is the first texture to be described.

Homophonic Texture

In a **homophonic texture** (see Example 13.1) there is one **melodic line** and one or more other lines that serve to support and accompany the main melodic line. This is the prevailing texture of the common practice music, most popular music, and most vocal music. In the following example, an excerpt from a four-part **chorale** by **Bach**, the voices move together almost entirely with the same rhythm to form basic, **root position** chords that support the melody in the top voice.

Example 13.1
Homophonic texture: Bach, Chorale No. 14 "O Herre Gott, dein göttlich Wort", mm. 1–2

The only chord that is not completely obvious is the V^7 chord. Since there is a four-voice texture, as might often happen, Bach has left out the **fifth** of the V^7 chord and uses two **roots** instead, but it is easy to hear and analyze this as a V^7 chord nonetheless.

The term **harmonic rhythm** describes the most common durational value of each **harmony** in a passage. In this case, the harmonic rhythm is the quarter note. The harmonic rhythm will not always be the same durational value throughout a passage as it is in Example 13.1. In fact, in most pieces of music it will vary. The chorale in Example 13.2 has a more complex texture, but as you listen to it, notice how the chord changes are primarily on the quarter note in the first measure, and on the half note in the second measure.

Example 13.2
Bach, Chorale No. 22 "Schmücke dich, o liebe Seele", mm. 4–5

Although there are constant eighth notes occurring in the first measure, the harmonic rhythm is only a quarter note value. Some of these eighth notes do not seem to fit the chords formed by the other notes and are heard as **dissonant**. These are called **non-chord tones** or **embellishing tones**, and are circled in Example 13.3.

Example 13.3
Bach: Chorale No. 22 "Schmücke dich, o liebe Seele", mm. 4–5

When non-chord tones are removed, the harmonic analysis becomes much easier, as shown in Example 13.4. This is called a **harmonic reduction**.

Example 13.4
Harmonic reduction of Example 13.2

In a harmonic reduction, the rhythm is simplified and notes that are not part of the essential **harmony** are eliminated. This does not mean they are not important: notice how most of these extra notes serve to help smooth out the individual lines by filling in the **melodic intervals** between the rather blocky chords in the reduction, making the passage more musical. However, when analyzing music it is helpful to focus on one aspect at a time, in this case the harmony, and to remove the other elements so that the aspect being examined is more clear.

In keyboard music written for non-sustaining instruments such as the piano and harpsichord, or plucked instruments such as guitar and harp, the **chorale** style does not work as well, since the sound dies away quickly. Or, in orchestral music, the composer might wish to add more rhythmic energy than the stately, reverent, chorale style allows. Example 13.5 shows one way a piece can sustain energy in chords using what is termed a **blocked chord style**.

In the first measure, the A minor **i** chord is performed as eighth-note blocked chords. In the second measure, the same chord is sustained in the lower three voices while the melody continues in eighth notes (non-chord tones are circled). This basic alternation of block chording continues in the next six measures. When analyzing music in this style, the **Roman numeral** is only added when the **harmony** changes. Notice that this results in a two-measure **harmonic rhythm** that quickens to one measure only at the end of the passage. For music in a faster **tempo**, it is common to see harmonic rhythms extend to longer and longer values.

Example 13.5
Block chord style: Beethoven, *Russian Folk Song*, Opus 96 mm. 1–8

Another very common style in keyboard and instrumental ensemble music uses a technique called **arpeggiation** where the accompaniment plays the individual notes of a chord in succession melodically rather than all at once. When played rapidly enough, the chord tones are aurally grouped together and perceived to form a chord. When this occurs, the lowest note of the arpeggiation is used as the bass note to determine the **inversion**, as shown in Example 13.6.

Example 13.6
Use of arpeggiation with reduction: Mozart, Sonata K. 545, Mvt. I, mm. 63–66

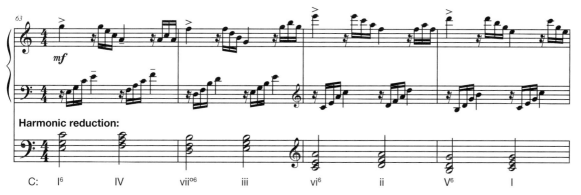

A popular technique of arpeggiating the chord alternates between chord tones in the pattern "bottom–top–middle–top", and is commonly referred to as **Alberti bass**. This is the technique used in our now-familiar Mozart example, shown in Example 13.7. If all of the notes in the pattern are grouped together into a single chord covering that duration, a block chord **harmonic reduction**, shown below the example, is often easier to analyze.

A third style of arpeggiation is called **broken chord style**, where two or more chord tones are arpeggiated over a wider range than the tightly spaced Alberti bass. Example 13.8 is a beautiful example of broken chord style by Chopin in his Opus 9, No. 2 (**opus numbers**

Example 13.7
Use of Alberti bass: Mozart, Sonata K. 545, Mvt. I, mm. 1–4

Harmonic reduction: (smaller notes are found in the melody)

are in order of the dates a composer wrote a work, and are used to help identify multiple works with the same title; "Opus 9" means that this set of Nocturnes was Chopin's ninth composition), but the harmonic analysis includes some chords that you may not yet recognize. This will often happen as you analyze music. When this happens, simply put the **pop/jazz chord symbol** under the harmony, as shown. If you recognize a **non-chord tone**, circle it.

Example 13.8
Use of broken chord style arpeggiation: Chopin, Nocturne Opus 9, No. 2, mm. 1–2

You may encounter other forms of arpeggiation, and these can be analyzed in a similar manner. There may also be an occasional **embellishing** tone in the pattern, but you can usually recognize these by the fact that they are fewer and "don't fit" in with all the other notes. Embellishing tones are not included in a harmonic reduction.

Monophonic Texture

In a **monophonic texture** there is only one line of music. An unaccompanied solo song would be one obvious example. However, if a large choral group is singing the same melody, even in different octaves, this is still considered a monophonic texture. Even though there is only one melodic line, chords may be outlined or suggested by a melody alone. In fact, most melodies in the common practice era are structured so as to express the underlying harmony. Generally speaking, notes that occur on strong beats imply the chords that would fit underneath them. These harmonies are often incomplete, and are called **implied harmony**. One of the most famous, largely monophonic examples from the common practice period comes, again, from the music of **J.S. Bach**. The Six Suites for Solo Cello contain passages that are most often monophonic (Bach uses a technique of playing on more than one string of the 'cello at once, called **multiple stops**, to compose some passages that are not monophonic. The last note of the following example is an example of this).

Frequently, monophonic passages will alternate between arpeggiated patterns and scale patterns. The notes occurring on beats are often heard more prominently and may form a part of the implied chord. If the notes on these strong beats fit a surrounding implied chord, they may be interpreted harmonically, but if not, they can be identified simply by **scale** type and key. When a pattern changes, this is sometimes an indication of a change in harmony as well. The first eight measures of the third movement of Bach's Suite for Solo 'Cello No. 1 are shown in Example 13.9, which demonstrate many of these analytical techniques.

Example 13.9
Bach, Suite for Solo 'Cello No. 1, Mvt. 3, mm. 1–8

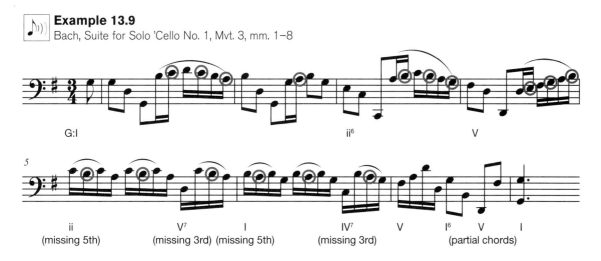

In the first four measures, there are arpeggiated eighth notes followed by scale passages. Notice, however, that if the sixteenth notes occurring on the eighth note pulse are kept, and the weaker sixteenth notes are considered **non-chord tones** (circled) there is a clear harmonic reduction to easily recognized chords occurring one per measure. In the fifth and sixth measures, the pattern is the same on the first two beats and changes on the third. If the weak "B" sixteenth notes in measure 5 and the weak "A" sixteenth notes in measure 6 are circled and excluded, and the lowest notes used as the root of the implied chords, a **harmonic structure** begins to emerge. Then, notice how Bach directly outlines them (incompletely) via arpeggiation in measure 7, leading to a firm arrival on **tonic** in measure 8.

Polyphonic Texture

Polyphonic texture is that in which all of the **voices** function more melodically than harmonically. Each line has an independent identity that the composer carefully crafts to fit with the other lines on a moment-to-moment basis called **counterpoint**. Although there will be brief passages where there is a clear harmony implied or directly stated, a harmonic analysis of most polyphonic music is difficult and often not very fruitful. Polyphonic music frequently changes the sense of tonic to different keys, a technique called **modulation**. Although a thorough coverage of this technique is beyond the scope of this text, a modulation can be recognized by a sustained, consistent use of an **accidental** or a change of the **key signature** that changes our perception of what pitch is tonic. When a consistent, new accidental is combined with the original key signature, this will usually form a new major or minor (melodic or harmonic) scale that can be identified and labeled. More simple polyphonic music might closely resemble the **chorale** form in Example 13.2, and if so, this may be harmonically reduced and analyzed. Otherwise, for now it is best to simply identify it as "polyphonic" and focus on identifying the use of themes and **motives** (both melodic and rhythmic), identifying the key in which they occur. Example 13.10 shows the opening phrase of Bach's Two-Part Invention No. 1. The principal motif is identified for you. Can you find all of the places he uses it? (Analyzing counterpoint can be like a "find the word" puzzle. Sometimes the theme is in another form: upside-down, backwards, etc.)

 Example 13.10
Bach, Two-Part Invention No. 1, mm. 1–7

13.2 Melodic Analysis

Melodic analysis consists of recognizing and labeling patterns and traits used in the melodic line. Much of this has been covered in previous chapters: rhythmic motives (**Chapter 2**), scales (**Chapters 6** and **7**), intervals (**Chapter 10**) and in this chapter, arpeggiation and harmonic implications. Two more elements may be also identified that provide insight into melodies: **phrase** and **melodic contour**.

Phrase

Just as in spoken languages, the **tonal** musical language has points of forward motion and meaning, and points of rest or pause. In written English, punctuation (such as a comma or period) indicates both a slight pause and a division of a sentence into phrases. In music, melodies also have points of motion and rest. The general term of a point of rest or pause is called a **cadence**. Although there are many types that will be studied and defined in your future music theory studies, the basic concept of a cadence is really quite simple. A longer note duration occurring at the end of a musical passage that frequently is followed by a short rest causes a sense of cadence. Repetition of similar material can also cause us to hear each statement as a separate phrase separated by a weaker form of a cadence, what in written English might be analogous to two phrases separated by a comma. (Just like the previous sentence, in fact!) Many musicians and theorists have remarked that a cadence is one of the easiest things in music to hear, but one of the hardest things to verbally define. A basic way to begin analyzing melodies is to mark the obvious cadences as you hear them. Then label them as **conclusive** if it sounds like the music comes to a stopping point (like a period or exclamation point in English) or if it is **inconclusive** if the music comes to an important moment but couldn't "end" at that point. Listen to Example 13.11 and try pausing the playback at the point marked as an inconclusive cadence. Notice how incomplete it sounds and how hard it is *not* to want to click the play button again! Then, click play and notice how "final" the conclusive cadence at the end sounds.

Although a harmonic analysis of this example would be difficult and beyond the level of this course, the phrases are identifiable, and analyzing the use of rhythmic motives gives much to discuss.

Example 13.11
Principal cadences: Chopin, Prelude Opus 28, No. 20

Melodic Contour

Most phrases have a basic, overall shape that helps to define the character of a passage. Take for example our familiar **Mozart** melody from the first movement of his Symphony No. 40 in G minor, shown in Example 13.12.

Example 13.12
Melodic contours: Mozart, Symphony No. 40, Mvt. I, mm. 1–16

Although there will usually be some "zig-zags" in the actual melody, the basic, overall **contour** of most common practice **phrases** falls into one of four basic types, shown in Example 13.13.

Example 13.13
Basic contour types for musical phrases

Once phrases are identified, the **contour** can also be labeled. Each contour has its own character, and composers recognize this and use it in their compositions to convey different moods and senses of energy and motion. Rarely will a melody have a "flat-line" contour. In fact, flat-line's in the contour of melodies written by young composers will often elicit the same response from their teachers as a medical doctor: "I'm sorry . . . it's dead."

13.3 Further Thoughts on Analysis

Although music studies often select examples that clearly demonstrate the topics discussed, music is an art and, as such, rarely follows the rules strictly. When approaching a work in analysis, a measure of flexibility is required. Often, the most wonderful moments in music are when a composer "bends" the rules, and creates an unexpected moment that surprises the listener. This does not make analysis a futile effort. Rather, it is through analysis that these exceptions and atypical moments are made more clear, which allows performers to approach them in more musically informed manners and listeners to better appreciate them more and more with each listening.

Chapter Summary

Harmonic rhythm describes the most common durational value of each harmonic change in a passage. In a **harmonic reduction**, the rhythm is first simplified to the harmonic rhythm and notes that are not part of the essential harmony (called **non-chord tones** or **embellishing tones**) are eliminated. This allows for easier identification of the chords using Roman numerals, or if some of the **Roman numerals** cannot be determined by using **pop chord symbols**, as a starting point for further analysis.

There are three basic **textures** that describe most of the music of the common practice period. **Monophonic** textures consist of a single **voice** (which may be doubled by several voices or instruments) and often outline incomplete **implied harmonies**. **Homophonic** textures use one melodic line and one or more other lines that serve to support and accompany the main melodic line. This is the prevailing texture of the common practice music, most popular music, and much vocal music. Homophonic textures often use **arpeggiation** patterns, such as **Alberti bass** or **broken chords** or use **blocked chord style** to add energy to the accompaniment. **Polyphonic** textures use multiple melodic lines that are written in a style called **counterpoint**, where each line has its own independence and identity, but all fit together on a moment-to-moment basis. Harmonic analysis is less effective for much of the music in polyphonic examples, which use **motives** and **modulation** to other tonal centers to a greater degree.

Melodic analysis identifies rhythmic **motives**, **scales**, and **melodic intervals**, as well as the identification of **phrases** and **contours**. **Phrases** are musical passages that are separated by **cadences**, which are brief pauses or interruptions of the forward motion, similar to punctuation marks in written English. They generally fall into two broad categories: **conclusive cadences** and **inconclusive cadences**. Phrases are generally one of four very basic **contour types: arch, inverted arch, ascending ramp**, and **descending ramp.**

Although the study of music fundamentals and theory usually presents examples that use the techniques in a clear and simple manner, music is an art, and when analyzing one should take an open, flexible approach, looking for the exceptions and variances that help create some of the most wonderful moments in this much loved art form.

Chapter 13 Exercises

The following is the complete first movement from Mozart's Piano Sonata in
C Major K. 545, which has been featured frequently in excerpts throughout this
text. As both a final review and a synthesis of all that has been studied, first listen
to this work all the way through (several times if possible) then identify and label
as many of the musical elements as you can: begin with textures, principle
cadences, and phrases. Then within these elements, look for rhythmic motives,
use of scales, specific interval use that is interesting, and any other details you
can find that bring out some kind of a relationship to you. Does any musical
material repeat? Does it repeat exactly? If not, how does it differ? Are there
places where the music seems to be in a key not suggested by the key
signature? Start with the large ideas and work your way down to the details—
there is more than enough to keep a diligent student engaged for much longer
than the time you will likely have. As a class, bring all of your findings together
and see what others have found in addition to your analysis.

Music Notation and Calligraphy

Clear, correct music notation is something most musicians take for granted. Publishers have spent much time perfecting the guidelines of how music is typeset, and often these details go unnoticed. Music notation software has taken some of the burden of music notation off the shoulders of musicians, but even these fine programs will only do what the human enters. There are many helpful guides available, and every musician should own one and refer to it any time there is a question about how to notate something. In the absence of a reference book, one may also refer to a modern score of a similar work published by a reputable publisher. Many early scores typeset in the nineteenth century contain notational errors, and should be avoided. Regardless of advances in music software, every musician will have to write music by hand (including your assignments in this text) and, for the sake of the musicians who will be reading your music (and your instructor!), clear, accurate music notation and penmanship—called **music calligraphy**—are essential skills.

Musical notation is based on straight, vertical lines and horizontal elements set mainly on a 30 degree angle. Vertical lines are always exactly vertical, however **noteheads** and **accidentals** are not "level" but incline at approximately a 30 degree angle:

Example A1.1
30 degree angle in music calligraphy

Key signatures also are arranged along this same angle. **Sharps** are arranged in an inclining angle, while **flats** are arranged along similarly declining angles. Note the precise spacing and arrangement and position of accidentals in each **clef** (Example A1.2).

Clefs are often difficult to draw in a proper shape and proportion. Calligraphers use primarily downward strokes, letting the pen or pencil drag along rather than "push" across the paper, and this leads to a smoother, more well-controlled line. Example A1.3 shows a step-by-step approach to drawing clefs. Notice how all strokes are primarily downward.

Example A1.2
Key signature notation

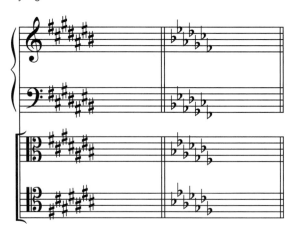

Thick lines can be drawn easily with two side-by-side downward strokes (alto clef step 1). The final step in each, shaping, is optional. For alto clefs (or tenor clef or any of the "C" clefs) in hand manuscript, an optional "K Clef" is commonly accepted. It uses a simpler, non-shaped clef design that still provides a clear indication of the line corresponding to **Middle C**. As with any skill, practice with a printed clef for reference makes perfect.

Example A1.3
Drawing clefs

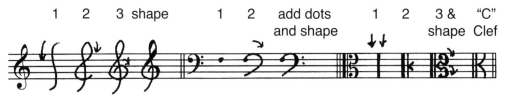

A simple trick to create smooth, properly shaped **noteheads** is shown in Example A1.4. The three steps are: a) begin at the center (on the line, or centered in the space), b) "spin" it outward, spiraling clockwise if you are right handed, counterclockwise if left handed, and c) gradually build up the shape of the notehead to the correct size and angle. Do not try to draw a circle and scribble it in.

Example A1.4
Drawing filled noteheads

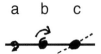

Whole notes are the only noteheads that do not angle upwards. All others do. **Half notes** may be shaded on the upper left and lower right sides by simply applying a little more pressure to the page with the pen or pencil to widen the line. Vertical **stem** lines are about one octave in length and should be drawn with a very light touch to make them as thin as possible: be sure your pencil is sharp! Notes above the middle line of the **staff** have downward **stems**; notes below the middle line have upward stems; those on the middle line, or in **beamed** groups that are on both sides of the middle line, may go either direction, whatever looks best with the music around it. They must be perpendicular to the staff lines and straight—here is where a credit card or ID with the raised letters facing *downward* (this prevents smearing from underneath by raising the edge of the card off the paper) is one of the best tools. The lower or upper edge can be lined up with a staff below or above to help create a 90 degree angle to the staff lines. Example A1.5 shows two ways of drawing **flags**: both are acceptable. Shaped **flags** attempt to mimic the printed flag shape while "straight flags" are shorter, thick, straight lines that angle inward. Notice that ALL flags go on the right side of the stem regardless of if the stem is up or down. As more flags are added, stem lengths may be lengthened. In all cases, downward strokes are usually smoother and easier to draw.

Example A1.5
Drawing notes and rests

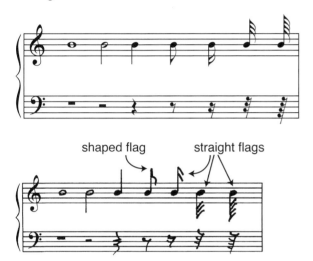

When notating **seconds** and clusters (a series of adjacent seconds), the note at the end of the stem is always in the correct position and alignment with other notes in other staves. Notate the end note first, then add the additional notes to alternating sides of the stem as needed. The lower note of a second is always to the left of the upper. **Accidentals** are added from top to bottom, unless there are more than three or space allows for the lower ones to fit closer to the **noteheads** underneath the upper accidentals. The basic principle of clusters is to make it as clear and clean as possible, with all accidentals directly on the same line or space as the notehead they alter (see Example A1.6).

Example A1.6
Seconds and clusters

Beaming should always match the **time signature**. In **common time**, notes are sometimes beamed in two-beat groupings at faster **tempi**. However, either method, shown in Example A1.7, is correct. Beams are thick, straight (use your card!) and connect outer note stems. Try not to make any note stem within a beam shorter than a **fifth**, or longer than a **thirteenth** if possible.

Example A1.7

Beaming

2-beat "common line" beaming standard beat beaming

In a four-voice SATB (soprano, alto, tenor, bass) **chorale** style, as is used for many music theory exercises, the soprano and alto are always notated on the treble clef staff, and the tenor and bass always on the bass clef staff. Each keeps separate stems, with soprano always up, alto always down, tenor always up, and bass always down. In any **texture** or number of **voices**, **beaming** and **ties** always break between weak to strong **beats**, but may cross between strong to weak **beats** (see alto, measure 1 and soprano, measure 2 in Example A1.8).

Example A1.8

Breaking ties in a four-voice texture and beams across weak-to-strong beats in a two-voice texture

Example A1.9 demonstrates several common notational errors in the upper staff, and the corrected notation below.

1. Unneeded **tie** across beats 1 and 2. A dotted value is cleaner. However, a **dotted** value is normally not used between beats 2 and 3 in **triple** meters.

2. **Beaming** does not match the **time signature**.

3. Multi-beat **tuplets** may only cross from strong to weak beats, just like beaming. Otherwise they must be broken. Tuplets may not be **syncopated**.

4. Whole rests in empty **measures** are the only rhythmic notation which is centered in the measure. All other single notes or rests must occur on beat one at the beginning of the measure.

Example A1.9

Common errors and corrections

Dynamics are always centered below, or above in vocal music, the notehead to which they apply. One cannot have a "forte rest." All dynamic markings, including **hairpins** and text, should be lined up on each staff system. In notation software, always attach dynamics to the note, not the staff, whenever possible, as this will insure that they always line up correctly even when respacing.

Notation software will draw **dynamic** markings properly, but in hand manuscript it should be noted that, for example, a mezzo-forte is not just the letters "mf" but rather, the characters are stylized, shaped characters. The "f" is actually more like the sound holes on a violin. In manuscript, however, simply writing them as italicized letters that attempt to match the published shape is usually acceptable.

Slurs connect the *outsides* of the **noteheads** they cover, while **ties** connect the *insides* of the noteheads they join. Slurs should go on the opposite side of the **stems**, and in cases with mixed stem direction or if a slur would overlap with dynamics, etc., they should go on whichever side results in the most clean, clear notation. These guidelines are demonstrated in Example A1.10, which also shows the proper placement of dynamics, hyphenated text, word extension lines (when a syllable extends over several notes), and the breaking of beams when a new syllable of text begins.

Example A1.10
Vocal and instrumental use of dynamics

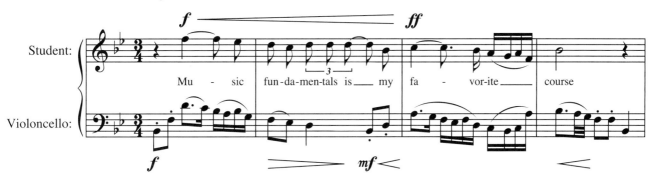

Notice also in this example the importance of vertical alignment of all **beats**, **divisions**, and **subdivisions**. Although notation software does this automatically, when writing music by hand, it is very important to be sure notes in all staves line up vertically according to their beats, divisions, and subdivisions. Music is a graphical notation, and when notes do not properly line up vertically, musicians will have great difficulty playing the passage. It may help to notate the part with the most divisions and subdivisions first, then align the simpler parts to that. Example A1.11 combines a number of common manuscript errors and shows how by using a straight-edge (such as a credit card) and lining up notes, the passage becomes much more clear and easy to read.

These are only a few general, starting guidelines to help you begin. As you read professionally typeset music, pay particular attention to the spacing, placement, shape, and layout of the music, and work toward incorporating as many of these traits into your own music calligraphy and notation.

Example A1.11

Proper vertical alignment of notes and general neatness issues

Misaligned notes, crooked lines, and misshaped notes:

Correct alignment, straight vertical lines, and proper shapes:

The Overtone Series and Consonance vs. Dissonance

Many of the fundamental principles in **tonal** music are based on acoustics and the mathematical relationships between tones. Numerous books have been written on the topic of musical acoustics, but one fundamental aspect, the **overtone series**, defines and explains how and why our tonal system of music works. A basic understanding of this topic is essential not only for understanding music fundamentals and theory, but also orchestration, tuning, balance, and how most acoustic instruments function. The principles and mathematics are simple, but the application is far reaching.

The Overtone Series

As noted in **Chapter 3**, an **octave** consists of two **pitches** whose **frequencies** are in the ratio of 1:2 (i.e. A3 = 220 Hz and A4 = 440 Hz). The A4, being a perfect multiple (two times the frequency, or 2x) of A3, acoustically reinforces it, resulting in what is called a **perfect consonance**. Example A2.1 shows the relationship between two frequencies that are in this 1:2 relationship. For every cycle of the 1x frequency, there are two perfect cycles

Example A2.1
The 1:2 Frequency relationship forming the octave

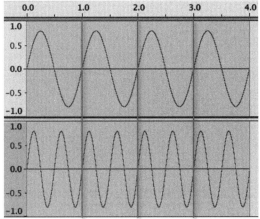

Frequency 1x (top) and 2x (bottom)

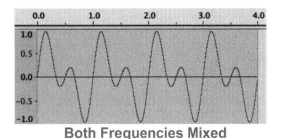

Both Frequencies Mixed

of the 2x frequency and when mixed together (shown in the second waveform) notice how they form one consistent waveform with characteristics of both. The audio example plays first the 1x tone, then the 2x tone, then both mixed.

This relationship between pitches whose frequencies are perfect multiples of each other explains the principle of **octave equivalence**.

The original, lowest frequency (1x) is called the **fundamental**. Each multiple of the frequency above the fundamental is called an **overtone**. All multiples of the fundamental, including the fundamental itself (which is a 1x multiple) are also called **harmonics**. Example A2.2 lists the first fourteen overtones above the pitch C2. As you play the example, note that some of the overtones are slightly out of tune with our Western tuning scales. These pitches are shown in parentheses.

Example A2.2

The overtone series to the fourteenth overtone

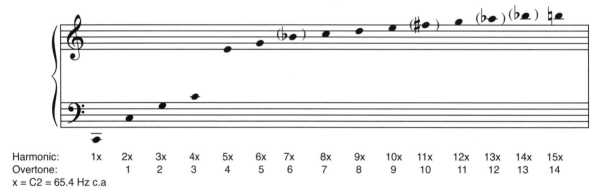

Harmonic:	1x	2x	3x	4x	5x	6x	7x	8x	9x	10x	11x	12x	13x	14x	15x
Overtone:		1	2	3	4	5	6	7	8	9	10	11	12	13	14

x = C2 = 65.4 Hz c.a

Brass instrument players may recognize this pattern and how it relates to their fingerings/slide positions, since it is the basis for how these instruments are constructed. String instruments and some woodwind instruments are able to play harmonics, which are directly derived from the first five overtones in the series.

In fact, almost every aspect of our modern music making has some relevance to the overtone series. This is no coincidence, and the early musicians who developed the tonal system over hundreds of years all studied the overtone series and applied it to the formation of our common practice **tonal** system.

Consonance and Dissonance

A look at the **interval** between each note of the overtone series (reducing those greater than an octave) reveals that the **perfect intervals** of P8 and P5 are closest to the

Example A2.3

Intervals within the overtone series

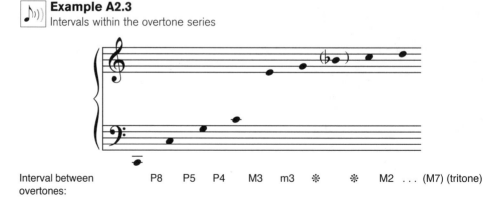

Interval between overtones:		P8	P5	P4	M3	m3	✳	✳	M2	. . .	(M7)	(tritone)

✳ not in tune

fundamental. Because there is a more simple mathematical relationship between their frequencies, they are heard as the most **consonant**. As overtones move farther away from the fundamental, the ratios and relationships between frequencies become more complex, and these are heard as less consonant or more **dissonant**.

Example A2.4 provides a chart of these intervals (along with their **inversions**) sorted by their distance away from the fundamental. Since the **tritone** does not appear in tune within the series, it is the most removed or dissonant interval.

Example A2.4
Chart of consonant and dissonant intervals

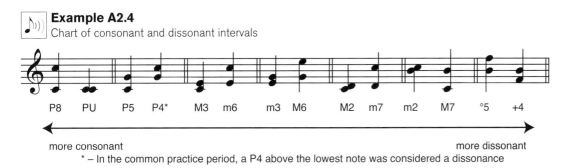

P8 PU P5 P4* M3 m6 m3 M6 M2 m7 m2 M7 °5 +4

more consonant   more dissonant
* – In the common practice period, a P4 above the lowest note was considered a dissonance

As you listen to each of these being played, try to imagine if that interval could serve as a stable, final sound in **common practice** music. In tonal music, the more consonant intervals are also heard as the more stable intervals. Many people generally refer to intervals beyond the minor third and major sixth (including all **seconds**, **sevenths**, and the **tritone**) as dissonant, and intervals before the minor sixth as consonant, but it is perhaps more helpful to think of this as a gradual change from "more consonant" to "more dissonant."

Over the centuries, people's tastes and perceptions of what point constitutes the break between "consonant" and "dissonant" has changed. In the year 1200, for example, only perfect octaves and perfect fifths were considered consonant, and the tritone was commonly referred to as the *diabolus in musica* ("devil in music") and was strictly avoided. From about 1300 on, thirds and sixths began to be considered consonant, but fourths were not. During the early common practice, the division occurred after the minor sixth, but the perfect fourth was still considered dissonant when it occurred above the **bass**, because it was heard as needing to resolve down to a third! However, since the late 1900s most classical music and jazz has made frequent use of all intervals, with even tritones heard as pleasant, final sonorities.

Regardless of one's personal taste, the overall relative stability/instability of these intervals is founded in the physics and mathematics of the overtone series, and by understanding their relationships to one another, music of all periods can be better understood and appreciated.

Appendix Summary

The **overtone series** consists of a **note** called the **fundamental**, and a series of **pitches** whose **frequencies** are multiples of the fundamental called **overtones**. The first three overtones are most strongly related to the fundamental and are considered **perfect consonances**, since their frequencies most strongly fit and reinforce that of the fundamental. As overtones move farther away from the fundamental their relationships become less strong and more complex, and the interval between those overtones and the fundamental becomes more **dissonant**. The perception of what constitutes a consonance and what constitutes a dissonance has changed over time, and while the acoustic relationships remain the same, tastes and preferences have now expanded to allow use of all intervals.

Terms and Definitions

accidental   an alteration of the pitch by the addition of a symbol before the notehead to indicate the raising or lowering of the pitch by a prescribed number of half steps (as indicated by the type of symbol used). The following are examples of accidentals: sharps, flats, double sharps, double flats and naturals.

adagio   tempo marking meaning slowly, 55–72 beats per minute.

Aeolian   a seven-note scale consisting of the pattern: *whwwhww*. This scale is also referred to as the natural minor scale.

Alberti bass   a popular accompanimental pattern in which the notes of the chord are arpeggiated in the pattern of "bottom–top–middle–top."

allegro   tempo marking meaning fast, 115–142 beats per minute.

alto clef   one of the "C" clefs, with middle c (C4) centered on the middle line of the staff.

anacrusis   an incomplete measure at the beginning of a metered section of music. The total duration of the anacrusis (also commonly referred to as "pick ups") usually is deducted from the final measure of music.

analysis   the focused examination of various aspects of music to gain greater insight into its function, structure, and qualities.

andante   tempo marking meaning moderately slow, 72–90 beats per minute.

arpeggiation   where one voice or instrument plays the individual notes of a chord in succession.

articulations   symbols placed on notes to indicate a different attack or duration than would normally be given. Examples are accent, staccato, and legato markings. Articulations typically are placed next to the notehead on the opposite side of the stem.

asymmetrical   not symmetrical. Often used to refer to meters with an odd number (greater than three) of beats or subdivided beats, resulting in an uneven subdivision of the measure.

augmented   referring to either an interval that is one half step larger than a perfect or a major interval. An augmented triad (abbreviated Aug or "+") consists of a major third and an augmented fifth above the root (M3+M3). For rhythms, a proportional increase in the rhythmic values in a passage.

backslash   used in figured bass, a backslash through a number means to raise that corresponding note by a chromatic half step.

barline   a vertical line in the staff that delineates a complete measure.

Baroque   a period of time from approximately 1600 to 1750. Music of this period developed the principles and style now known as the common practice. Prominent composers of this period included Bach, Handel, Schütz, Vivaldi, Corelli, and Telemann.

bass clef (also known as the "F" clef)   a symbol added to a staff used to indicate the assignment of pitches, with middle C (C4) occurring on the first ledger line above the staff.

bass note or **bass line**   the lowest sounding note(s) of a series of chords, often heard along with the melody as most important. The bass note may or may not be the root of a chord and is used to determine the inversion of a chord.

beam(s)   line(s) connecting notes with a duration of an eighth note or shorter, that occur within the time of one beat. The number of beams is equal to the number of flags normally found on the note, so a group of eighth notes has a single beam, a grouping of sixteenth notes has two beams, etc. When there is a mixture of various note values, beams connect like note values that are next to each other and within the beat.

beat   a regularly occurring interval of time in metered music used to subdivide each measure. Also usually perceived as a consistent pulse.

beat groups   perceived associations of beats within each measure based on recurring patterns of strong (S) and or weak (W) beats. Basic patterns are comprised of groups of two (called a simple beat group) or three (called a compound beat group), with a strong beat on the first of the group.

beat note value   the rhythmic note value that receives the beat in common practice music. This will be a standard note value in simple meters and a dotted note value in compound meters.

blocked chord style   the repetition of a chord in a regular rhythm as a means of adding rhythmic energy to an accompaniment. Frequently used in piano and classical orchestral works.

cadence   a point of rest or pause in music, generally either conclusive or inconclusive.

cadenza   a free, solo passage that may or may not conform to a meter.

cautionary accidentals (also known as **courtesy accidentals**)   accidentals added in parenthesis as helpful reminders that the accidental in the previous measure is no longer applied.

chorale   a composition, usually four-voiced, that proceeds in a primarily homophonic texture with both harmonic progression and individual voice-leading having equal importance.

chord   a chord is a set of three or more pitches that sound at the same time or in succession as in an arpeggiation or other gesture. A triad is a chord consisting of three pitch classes that form two stacked thirds, and is the basis of tonal harmony.

chromatic   referring to letter note names that are altered by use of an accidental. When used in successive half steps, forms a chromatic scale.

chromatic half step   a half step where both notes use the same letter name (e.g. A-flat up to A-natural).

chromatic inflection   altering a solfege syllable in sight singing to accommodate an accidental.

circle of fifths   a memory aid listing all major and minor key signatures, with parallel relationships. Also relates to harmonic progressions where the root movement is up by perfect fifths.

clef   a clef is a symbol that is placed on a five-line staff to indicate what pitches are associated with each line and space of the staff (for examples, see: treble clef, alto clef, tenor clef, and bass clef).

close spacing   four-voiced, SATB (soprano, alto, tenor, bass) chords in which the soprano and tenor voices are less than an octave apart.

common practice period   a historical period of approximately 1650–1900. Music of this period and style functions in certain ways that best define our concept of tonal harmony. Although music written outside of this period (and some of the music written during this period) may not function completely according to the "rules" of tonal theory, it may have similar traits. Most tonal music today is strongly influenced by common practice music, and therefore a knowledge of it is essential for understanding many other styles of music.

common time   (**c time**) equivalent to $\frac{4}{4}$ meter.

compound groupings   beats that normally divide into three equal divisions (Sww).

compound interval   an interval that exceeds an octave in size.

compound meter   a meter that consist of compound beat groups. Beats in compound meters consist of dotted note values, so in a time signature for a compound meter, the top number specifies the number of divided beat notes (beats times three) and the bottom number specifies the divided (by three) beat note value.

consonance (opposite of **dissonance**)   relative terms that refers to how well two or more pitches "fit together." Consonant pitches have frequencies that are related to one another in simple ratios, while dissonant intervals have less related frequencies. Consonant intervals are found at the bottom of the overtone series, while more dissonant intervals exist between the fundamental and pitches higher up along the overtone series.

contour   a general term used to describe the overall shape of a melodic line. Usually one of four basic types: arch, inverted arch, ascending ramp, and descending ramp.

counterpoint   two or more voices that each have an individual, independent identities while fitting together intervalically on a moment to moment basis and tonally on a larger scale.

cut time   (¢ **time**) equivalent to $\frac{2}{2}$ meter.

diatonic   literally "between the two tonics." Generally refers to music that remains within the confines of an unaltered scale in a given key or mode.

diatonic half step   one in which each of the two notes has a different letter name (e.g. G-sharp up to A).

diminished   referring to an interval that is one half step smaller than a perfect or a minor interval. Also refers to a diminished triad (abbreviated dim or "°") consisting of a minor third and a diminished fifth above the root (m3+m3). For rhythms, a proportional decrease in the rhythmic values in a passage.

dissonant   a non-stable relationship between two or more notes that have frequencies that do not form simple ratios between their frequencies, resulting in a level of discord. In tonal music, dissonances serve to heighten tension and lead to satisfying resolutions. Although tastes have changed over time, dissonant intervals in common practice music are seconds, fourths, sevenths, and augmented or diminished intervals.

division   a first level breaking of a beat into equal parts. Simple meters divide into two equal parts, compound meters divide into three equal parts.

divisive rhythm   how note values in common practice music break into smaller divisions and subdivisions within a beat.

dominant   the scale degree name that refers to scale degree 5. Also refers to the triad built on the fifth scale degree (V). In minor keys, the dominant triad most often has a raised third (reflected in the harmonic minor form of the scale). This chord most often resolves to the tonic in tonal harmony.

dot   a dot following a notehead increases the note's duration by 50 percent.

double flat   ♭♭ a symbol that lowers the pitch or pitch class two half steps.

double sharp   x a symbol that raises the pitch or pitch class two half steps.

downbeat   the first beat of the measure, receiving a slight metric accent.

duple (two)   used in music to refer to a meter with two beats.

dynamics   symbols placed below (or above in choral/vocal music) notes to indicate how loud the music should be performed.

embellishment   the elaboration of a musical gesture or line through the addition of trills, stylistic patterns, and non-chord tones.

enharmonic   the relationship between two pitch classes that represent the same note, for example, G-sharp and A-flat. It may also help to think of it as two different letter names, with at least one requiring an accidental, that represent the same key on the piano.

equal temperament   a system of tuning the 12 half steps of a chromatic scale away from the natural tuning derived from the overtone series so that all perfect fifths are in tune with each other. This tuning system was developed during the common practice period to allow keyboard instruments to play in all major and minor keys.

fermata (⌢) informally called a "hold" or "birds-eye," indicating that the pulse and tempo stop for all parts for an interval of time determined by the performer if not specified. The length is usually proportionate to the length of the note or rest on which the fermata occurs.

figured bass a common notation system in Baroque music consisting of a bass note with small numbers and/or accidentals below the bass note called **figured bass symbols** which indicate the intervals of the pitches above that note. Keyboard players would then realize, or improvise an accompaniment, in a live performance above the bass line, which was played by another instrument. Both the bass instrument and keyboard realization together are called a **basso continuo**.

first inversion when a triad or seventh chord has the third of the chord as the lowest note (in the bass).

fixed "Do" solfege a sight singing system in which the pitch class "C" is always "do," where notes are sung according to their fixed names rather than according to their function.

flag a symbol that is attached to a note stem to designate rhythmic duration.

flat ♭ a symbol that lowers the pitch or pitch class one half step.

flat keys those key signatures with one or more flats in them.

fifth general interval for pitches four scale degrees apart. Interval quality commonly may be diminished, perfect, or augmented. Also refers to the chord tone in a triad or seventh chord a fifth above the root.

forte (*f*) dynamic marking meaning "loud."

fortissimo (*ff*) dynamic marking meaning "very loud."

fourth general interval for pitches three scale degrees apart. Interval quality commonly may be diminished, perfect, or augmented.

frequency the measure of how many pulses of air are occurring per second. It is expressed in hertz (Hz). Higher frequencies are heard as a higher pitch, and lower are perceived as a lower pitch. The range of human hearing is approximately 20 Hz (lowest pitch) to 20,000 Hz (very highest pitch). The frequency of Middle C is 261.6 Hz.

fully diminished refers to a seventh chord containing a diminished triad and a diminished seventh. Notated by following a lower case Roman numeral with a small superscript circle: "°" before the "7".

fundamental the lowest note of the overtone series, perceived to be the actual "pitch."

general interval the space between two pitches measured according to the number of scale degrees between them (beginning with 1 = unison). Does not take into account chromatic alterations.

grand staff a grouping of a treble clef staff and a bass clef staff with a brace to form a two-staff set covering the most common range of pitches. This is used for keyboard music. Middle C (C4) occupies the single ledger line between the staves.

half diminished   refers to a seventh chord containing a diminished triad and a minor seventh. Notated by following a lower case Roman numeral with a small superscript circle with a slash through it: "ø" before the "7". In pop/jazz notation it is referred to as a minor seventh with a flatted fifth.

half step   the smallest interval used in common practice music. There are 12 equal half step divisions of the octave, forming a chromatic scale. The keys on a piano keyboard (both black and white) are each a half step apart. May be diatonic or chromatic. Size of the specific intervals minor second, augmented unison, and more rarely, the diminished unison.

harmonic interval   the interval formed by two simultaneously sounding pitches.

harmonic minor scale   seven-note pattern spanning an octave with the interval pattern *whwwh3h* (with the "3" representing an augmented second/three half steps). Based on the natural minor scale with a raised scale degree 7 to create the leading tone and used primarily for harmonic function in minor keys.

harmonic progression   a series of chords that follows principles and guidelines defined by the overtone series and traditions of the common practice period, generally within a tonal framework. This also is referred to as harmonic function. In the tonal system, progressions occur when root movements are the following general intervals:

- up by second

- down by third

- up by fourth (or down by fifth)

- except V and vii°, which do not resolve to iii (or III in minor).

harmonic reduction   the process of simplifying several notes or voices that are playing the same pitches over the same period of time into a block chord, eliminating non-chord tones, dynamics, etc. allowing for an easier analysis.

harmonic regression (or retrogression)   when a sequence of chords functions in opposition to the principles that govern conventional harmonic progressions.

harmonic rhythm   the most common durational value of each harmony in a passage. Informally, as the rate at which the chords change.

harmony   a general term referring to the simultaneously sounding pitches (chords) that are used in a work. In the most general sense, harmony refers to the types of chords used predominantly in a work, or the harmonic system (i.e. tonal or otherwise) that is used in a composition. Harmony is also used to refer to a specific chord or series of chords.

homophonic (texture)   one melodic line and one or more other lines that serve to support and accompany the main melodic line, usually in the same rhythm or harmonic pulse.

implied harmony   notes that occur on strong beats surrounded by, or outlining, other members of a chord, without actually stating overtly the harmony itself. May also refer to incomplete chords that in context imply a given harmony without stating it completely.

improvise   to perform music without the use of a fully written-out musical notation. Live realization of figured bass or pop/jazz chord symbols are two examples of this.

interval   the distance between two pitches. When in succession, they are referred to as a melodic interval, and when sounding simultaneously, a harmonic interval.

inversion   for chords: the term used to specify which chord tone is the lowest position (in the bass). Derived from figured bass, inversions are shown by numbers listing the intervals of pitch classes above the bass (not including any additional octaves that may be present). A complete list is shown in Table 12.2. For intervals: the process of raising the lower note by one octave, placing it above the original upper note. Inverted intervals have similar sounds and relationships due to octave equivalence.

Ionian   mode with a seven-note scale consisting of the pattern *wwhwwwh*. This scale is also referred to as the major scale.

key   refers to the tonal center of musical passage that adheres to a single mode, usually indicated by a tonic pitch and mode or key signature. Also refers to the mechanical white and black "buttons" on a musical keyboard.

keyboard   a musical device spanning one or more octaves with seven larger white keys for the diatonic letter name notes and five smaller black chromatic keys per octave.

key signature   an ordered pattern of up to seven sharps or flats after the clef at the beginning of a staff that applies those accidentals to all pitch classes until cancelled. Used to include all accidentals found in major and minor keys.

key signature tool   a memory aid based on the order of sharps in the key signature that lists all keys and the number of sharps or flat in them. The following are illustrations of the Major and the Minor Key Signature Tools:

The Major Key Signature Tool:

	(F♯)	(C♯)					
Sharps:	6	7	1	2	3	4	5
	F	C(0)	G	D	A	E	B
Flats:	1	7	6	5	4	3	2
		(C♭)	(G♭)	(D♭)	(A♭)	(E♭)	(B♭)

The Minor Key Signature Tool:

	(F♯)	(C♯)	(G♯)	(D♯)	(A♯)		
Sharps:	3	4	5	6	7	1	2
	F	C	G	D	A(0)	E	B
Flats:	4	3	2	1	7	6	5
					(A♭)	(E♭)	(B♭)

largo   tempo marking meaning very slowly, 40–55 beats per minute.

leading tone   the scale degree name that refers to scale degree 7 in major, harmonic minor, and ascending melodic minor. A half step below tonic.

ledger lines   short lines used to extend the range of a staff beyond its normal five lines. Ledger lines are added according to the same spacing that the staff used. Several may be added according to the needs of the music, but if more than three ledger lines are consistently used, a change of clef is generally employed.

letter names   A, B, C, D, E, F, and G, used to refer to the unaltered, diatonic pitch classes on a staff in common practice music.

major   general usage: "larger/greater." Abbreviated Maj or "M". For interval quality: seconds (M2 = two half steps), thirds (M3 = four half steps), sixths (M6 = nine half steps), and sevenths (M7 = eleven half steps). For chords: triads consisting of two successive, stacked thirds with a major third on the bottom and a minor third on top (M3+m3).

major scale   seven-note pattern spanning an octave with the interval pattern *wwhwwwh*. Derived from the Ionian mode.

measure   a division of notated music according to the number of beats or divisions of the beat, as indicated by the time signature is generally employed. Measures are separated by a line through the staff called a barline.

mediant   the scale degree name that refers to scale degree 3.

melodic interval   an interval formed between two successive pitches.

melodic minor scale   seven-note pattern spanning an octave that alters a natural minor scale by raising scale degrees 6 and 7 on passages that ascend to tonic, and lowers them to their natural minor state on the descending passages. In so doing, this scale combines the functionality of the leading tone (ascending) and lowered submediant (descending).

melody   a successive line of notes heard as the primary material in a musical work, often in the uppermost voice.

meter   an organization of beats into groupings of two or three divisions and indicated by a time signature. The meter indicates the number of beats or divisions of a beat in each measure and also indicates which beats receive a slight emphasis.

metric transcription   the renotating of a passage from simple into compound time, converting normal divisions into tuplets and vice-verse.

metric transposition   the renotating of a musical passage that changes the beat note value and retains the proportion of all notes, so that if the beat note tempo remains the same, the rewritten passage will sound exactly like the original. Often used to simplify a passage rhythmically.

metronome   a device that provides a precise visual and/or aural reference for tempo. It can be set to an exact number of beats per minute and modern electronic versions allow for aural/visual divisions and subdivisions of the beat.

mezzo-forte (*mf*)   dynamic marking meaning "medium loud."

mezzo-piano (*mp*)   dynamic marking meaning "medium soft."

microtone   an interval smaller than a half step.

middle C   the pitch C4, frequency = 261.6 Hz, which is roughly in the middle of a piano keyboard and occupies the ledger line in the middle of a grand staff.

minor   general usage: "smaller/lesser." Abbreviated min or "m." For interval quality: seconds (m2 = one half step), thirds (m3 = three half steps), sixths (m6 = eight half steps), and sevenths (m7 = ten half steps) that are a chromatic half step smaller than their major counterparts. For chords: triads consisting of two successive, stacked thirds with a minor third on the bottom and a major third on top (m3+M3).

minor scale   derived from the Aeolian mode (*whwwhww*), consisting of three forms: natural, harmonic, and melodic.

mixed meter   music that contains multiple, changing time signatures.

mode   a seven-note scale spanning an octave. There are seven common modes which are each formed by beginning on a different line or space of the staff and using no accidentals.

moderato   tempo marking meaning moderately, when by itself 90–115 beats per minute. When following another tempo marking, meaning "a bit slower than" that tempo's normal speed.

modulation   a change in the perception of what pitch class is tonic within a composition, usually resulting in a cadence in that new tonal center.

monophonic texture   music consisting of only one line of music either as a solo or as a unison passage.

movable "do" solfege   a method of sight singing where the tonic pitch in major keys is always "do" and all other syllables move relative to this point of reference, emphasizing function over fixed pitch identities. In minor keys, there are two movable systems: 1) "La-based minor" is based on the relative minor relationship and bases all minor keys on the syllables for the relative major key (scale degree 6 in major, or "la"); and 2) "Do-based minor" uses the parallel relationship to a major key, and uses the same tonic ("do") and chromatic inflections to alter syllables.

music   music has been defined generally as "organized sound" and specifically so as to require an entire book to define. A general definition may best be defined as "sounds and pitches organized in time to create a chosen artistic or aesthetic statement." Music is both an art and a craft, based on acoustic principles, yet subject to various interpretations, hence its artistic merit.

musical notation   a system graphically representing organized sound. Common Practice music uses noteheads placed on a traditional five-line staff to convey pitch information. A system of various noteheads, flags, and beams is used to designate rhythm. Additional symbols exist for indicating dynamics, articulations, and other expressions needed for the composer to convey to the performer all of the information needed to realize the music.

natural   a symbol that cancels any previous accidentals and indicates that the plain, unaltered pitch class is to be used (i.e. C natural = "C").

natural minor scale   seven-note pattern with the interval pattern *whwwhww*. Derived from the Aeolian mode.

non-chord tones (embellishing tones)   notes which do not fit the chord, but are added by the composer to smooth out or embellish a line or to create harmonic dissonance and tension.

note   a single specified pitch or, in musical notation, a symbol specifying both pitch and rhythm.

notehead   a slanted oval used to indicate pitch and, according to its shape, duration.

octave   the relationship between two pitches in which one has a frequency of two times the other. Pitches in an octave equivalence have the same pitch class name, and when sounded together are perceived as the same pitch class. Also used to refer to different registers for specific pitches (e.g. octaves on the musical keyboard: C4 = Middle C, etc.).

octave equivalence   the principle, based on the relationship of the frequencies of pitches in the overtone series, that in musical analysis, pitch classes may be considered equal and reduced to a single, unspecified letter name (with accidental if needed).

open spacing   four-voiced, SATB (soprano, alto, tenor, bass) chords in which the soprano and tenor voices are an octave or more apart. Also often called "Keyboard Style" because of the ability to easily play the upper three voices in the right hand and the bass line in the left hand.

ottava symbol   ("Italian for "octave") used to specify that the given notes sound in a different octave than notated. *8va* indicates notes will sound one octave higher than notated. *15ma* indicates notes will sound two octaves higher than notated. *8vb* indicates notes will sound one octave lower than notated. *15^{mb}* indicates notes will sound two octaves lower than notated.

overtone   the series of overtones (exact multiples of the frequency of the fundamental pitch) are referred to as the *overtone series* and form the acoustical basis of tonal music.

parallel relationship   the relationship between major and minor keys that share the same tonic pitch (i.e. C major and c minor). Also called a change of mode.

perfect   interval qualities for unisons (PU = no half steps), fourths (P4 = five half steps), fifths (P5 = seven half steps), and octaves (P8 = 12 half steps).

"perfect pitch" (absolute pitch)   a trait in which people are able to recognize and sing pitches in tune without the need of an outside reference.

phrase   a passage in music that is normally separated by a cadence, and expresses a single (complete or incomplete) musical thought.

pianissimo (*pp*)   dynamic marking meaning "very soft."

piano (*p*)   dynamic marking meaning "soft."

pitch   refers to the highness or lowness of a sound which has a specific, single, steady, frequency. In common practice music, corresponding to one of 12 divisions of an octave and referred to by letter name and octave (i.e. C2).

pitch class   a general method of referring to all pitches which exist in an octave relationship. (i.e. C2, C4, and C7 are all pitch class "C").

polymeter   the simultaneous use of more than one time signature at once.

polyphonic   music in which all of the voices function more melodically than harmonically. Each line has an independent identity that the composer carefully crafts to fit with the other lines on a moment-to-moment basis called **counterpoint**.

pop/jazz chord symbols   symbols consisting of a pitch class letter name and symbols indicating the chord's quality, i.e. Cmaj7. Used to specify notes of a chord without any implication of harmonic function.

presto   tempo marking meaning very fast, 142+ beats per minute.

pulse   a regular, re-occurring emphasis of a fixed interval of time. Much like we feel our heart beat in a regular pulse, we often feel a regular beat or pulse in music.

quadruple   four. Used in music to refer to a meter with four beats.

quality the term added to general intervals, triads, and other chords specifying the exact interval sizes between pitches. Common qualities are major, minor, augmented, and diminished. For intervals: the quality precedes the general interval number, e.g. major second. For triads and seventh chords: the quality is determined by the specific types of thirds, e.g. a half-diminished seventh chord contains the following thirds: m3+m3+M3.

realization the working out of pitches from a figured bass notation, either in written form or improvised in live performance.

relative relationship the relationship between major and minor keys that share the same key signature. Relative minor keys have their tonic a minor third below their relative major keys and vice-verse.

resolution a note or chord that, according to its function, is expected to follow the previous chord or note. For example, scale degree 7 usually resolves to tonic, and a V chord that proceeds to a tonic chord is said to have resolved.

rest a symbol used to notate silence in musical notation.

rhythm a general term used to refer to the position of musical events in time. It specifies the beginning of an event and the duration (how long it lasts). When events occur in alignment to a regular interval of time, a "pulse" emerges. These pulses may be grouped into beats and measures, commonly called a meter. However, rhythms may occur freely in time as well.

rhythmic motive a recurring rhythm pattern that creates unity in a musical passage.

rhythmic reading a system of reading rhythms which uses numbers for beats and other syllables for divisions and subdivisions of the beat note type.

rhythmic reduction notation used for rhythmic analysis that eliminates pitch and only considers rhythm, usually notated on a one-line staff.

Roman numeral (analysis) traditional method of labeling chords according to their function, and uses Roman numerals corresponding to the scale degree of the root of the chord. These are followed by inversion symbols and may use upper or lower case and other symbols to indicate chord quality. Identifies chords as to their function in tonal music and only specifies pitches when combined with a tonal key.

root the lowest member of a triad, seventh chord, or any other chord, which forms the name and basis for the identity of that chord.

root position when a triad or seventh chord has the root of the chord as its lowest note. Considered to be the most stable form of a chord.

scale an ordered set of pitch classes that cover a range of one octave.

scale degree refers to the relative position of each successive letter-named note in the seven-note scale, with the first note of the scale being scale degree 1. The second note of the scale is scale degree 2, the third is scale degree 3, etc.

score a complete, written notation of a musical composition.

second general interval for pitches one scale degree apart. Interval quality commonly may be minor, major, or augmented.

second inversion   when triad or seventh chord has the fifth of the chord as the lowest note (in the bass).

semitone   another term for a half step.

seventh   general interval for pitches six scale degrees apart. Interval quality commonly is diminished, minor, or major. In seventh chords, used to refer to the note that is a seventh above the root.

seventh chord   series of stacked thirds forming a four-note chord.

sharp   ♯ a symbol that raises the pitch or pitch class one half step.

sharp keys   those key signatures with one or more sharps in them.

simple groupings   beats that normally divide into two equal divisions (Sw).

simple interval   an interval that is an octave or less in size.

simple meter   a meter that consist of simple beat groups. Beats in simple meters consist of standard note values, so in a time signature for a simple meter, the top number (usually 2, 3, or 4) specifies the number of beat notes and the bottom number specifies the beat note value (1 = whole note; 2 = half note; 4 = quarter note; 8 = eighth note, etc.).

sixth   general interval for pitches five scale degrees apart. Interval quality commonly is minor, major, or augmented.

solfege (solfegio)   a set of syllables (do-re-mi-fa-sol-la-ti/si) derived from the chant "*Ut queant laxis*" assigned to pitches or scale degrees as a means of teaching sight singing. This historical system is used in various forms around the world.

specific interval   measurement of the number of half steps between two notes by specifying the general interval preceded by a modifier indicating the interval's quality (perfect (P), major (M), minor (m), augmented (+), or diminished (°), and more rarely, double diminished (°°) and doubly augmented (++).

specific pitch   specifies both the pitch class and the octave in which it exists.

staff   a set of five lines with four spaces that are used in conjunction with a clef to provide a means of notating pitch. Noteheads are placed on the lines or spaces of the staff to notate pitch. Ledger lines may be used to extend the range of a staff.

stem   a small, thin line attached to a notehead and flag to help specify rhythm.

subdivision   the equal division (normally two parts) of the division of a beat.

subdominant   the scale degree name that refers to scale degree 4.

submediant   the scale degree name that refers to scale degree 6.

subtonic   the scale degree name that refers to scale degree 7 when it is a whole step below tonic in natural and descending melodic minor (lowered form of scale degree 7).

supertonic   the scale degree name that refers to scale degree 2.

system   each subsequent staff or group of staves in a score. Music is read on each staff until the right-hand margin, then resumes at the left side of the subsequent staff system.

tempo   a term used to describe at what rate the pulse or beat is occurring in a musical passage. Tempo may be indicated by such terms as "Allegro" (fast) or "Adagio" (slow) or more specifically in the number of beats per minute.

tendency tone   in functional tonality, a note separated by the interval of a diatonic half step from a more stable tone that has a musical "pull" toward that more stable tone. The leading tone is such a tendency tone, pulling up to tonic. Other diatonic tendency tones are scale degree 4 in major keys (pulling down to scale degree 3) and the lowered scale degree 6 in minor (pulling down to scale degree 5).

tenor clef   one of the "C" clefs, with middle C (C4) centered on the fourth line of the staff.

tertian   a harmony based on chords that are composed of stacked thirds. Derived from the overtone series, tertian harmony forms the basis for what we commonly call tonal music.

texture   how many voices there are in a passage of music and how the voices are arranged and relate to each other. Three basic textures describe most of the music of the common practice period: **monophonic**, **homophonic**, and **polyphonic**.

third   general interval for pitches two scale degrees apart. Interval quality commonly is minor or major. In triads and seventh chords, used to refer to the note that is a third above the root.

third inversion   when a seventh chord has the seventh as the lowest note (in the bass).

tie   a symbol added to connect two notes which combines their duration. A tie is a curved line that arcs on the opposite side of the notehead from the stem, and connects the insides of two and only two noteheads. If more than two notes need to be tied together, a separate tie is needed for each pair.

timbre   this term refers to the tone color or difference in the acoustic wave-shape of a sound. Examples of different timbres are a trumpet versus a flute or oboe playing the same passage.

time signature   a symbol occurring after the key signature consisting or two numbers, one above the other, used to indicate the meter. In simple meters, the top number refers to the number of beats, and the bottom number refers to beat note value. In compound meters, the top number refers to the number of divided beats and the lower number refers to the divided (by three) beat note value. Time signature remains in effect until cancelled or changed.

tonal   a hierarchy of pitches which functionally support or reference one pitch as the focal point or primary center, called the tonic. Based on acoustic principles and tradition, tonal harmony and theory has evolved into a structured musical language which was most commonly used during the common practice period.

tonal indexing   the visual and aural assignment of pitch and syllable to the notes to be sung prior to sight singing.

tonic   scale degree name that refers to scale degree 1. This is the primary pitch which functions as the focal point or primary center of a key in tonal music.

tonicization (pattern)   a musical scale or pattern used to orient the ear and eye to a new tonal center prior to sight singing a passage (tonal indexing).

transpose (transposition)   the changing of a pitch or set of pitches by raising or lowering it/them by a consistent general (diatonic transposition) or specific (chromatic transposition) interval.

transposing instrument   one built in a key other than "C" which will sound a pitch above or below the written/played pitch by a fixed interval.

treble clef (also called a "G" clef)   a symbol added to a staff used to indicate the assignment of pitches, with middle C (C4) located on the first ledger line below the staff. It is commonly paired with a bass clef to form a Grand Staff.

triad   a three-note chord composed of pitch classes that are each a third apart. The lowest pitch class of a triad is called the root. The names of other notes of the triad are derived from their interval above the root: the third and the fifth.

triple (three)   used in music to refer to a meter with three beats.

tritone   interval consisting of three whole steps (tri-tone) forming either an augmented fourth or diminished fifth. In early music (800–1600) was often avoided as it was considered to be the *diabolus in musica* ("devil in music").

tuplet   a non-standard subdivision of a beat or part of a beat (according to the meter) indicated by a beam or bracket and a small number indicating the total number of divisions.

unison   a general interval specifying that two pitches are notated on the same line or space on a staff. Perfect unisons (specific interval) also have the same chromatic inflection, resulting in the same pitch.

upbeat   the final, weak beat of each measure. Also used as an informal term for an anacrusis.

voice   in musical examples used not as a reference to the human voice, but to an individual part or line within a musical texture, regardless of what instrument or choral part is performing it.

whole step   an interval equal to two (2) half-steps, also known as a major second.

Supplemental Exercises for Sight Singing and Rhythmic Reading

These supplemental exercises are only intended as a starting point for further study. As class time permits, or for further study and practice after the completion of the course, these gradated exercises can be used to practice sight reading skills for both melody and rhythm. Students are strongly encouraged to integrate some sight singing into their daily practice, singing materials from their lessons and from the music played in their ensembles. The more the "inner ear" can imagine, hear, and then realize out loud accurate pitch and rhythm, the more fluently one is able to naturally "speak" the musical language.

Tonicization for major:

Tonicization for minor:

(Transpose to the key of the example to be sung.)

Indexing Exercises

To be sung in any clef and any key signature. Before singing, choose a key and clef, then tonicize in that key, visualizing the notes of the tonicization pattern prior to beginning. Once you are prepared, sing with a metronome, slowly and steadily at first, only working up to speed (approximately 132 beat per minute) when accuracy allows. You may begin or end at a note other than the first and last notes, as is musically appropriate.

1.

2.

Melodies in Major

Melodies in Minor

Rhythmic Exercises

1. Rhythmic Canon

Divide into four groups. All groups start at the beginning, one after the other as follows: each successive group begins when the first group has reached the point in the score with that group's number. (This is similar to the children's song "Row, Row, Row your Boat.")

Canon in 4 parts:

2. How to Perform 3 Against 2

To perform duplets (2) against triplets (3) the following exercise will help: count the rhythm listed below out loud as you first add your right hand tapping the top line (silently think the counts in parenthesis), repeating several times until that part is comfortable and secure. Then add the lower part. Continue repeating until secure. As a class, try to clap only one part (or divide into two groups, each performing one or the other parts), switching from one part to the other on cue from your instructor.

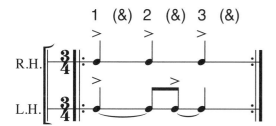

3. Duet Applying 2 against 3

One group claps and counts eighth notes while the other group accurately claps and counts the etude below. Then switch parts.

Group 1:

Group 2:

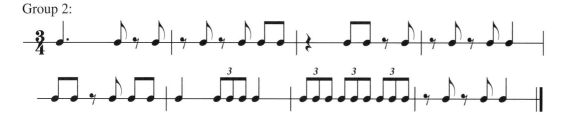

Index

accidental(s), 48*f*
  cautionary, 54, 54*f*
  courtesy, 54, 54*f*
  notating, 54, 54*f*
acoustic principles, 1
Adagio, 15
Aeolian mode, 61*f*, 70, 86
Alberti bass, 145
Allegro, 15
alto clef, 52*f*
  key signatures and, 82, 82*f*
anacrusis, 26–27
analysis(es)
  harmonic, 142–148
  melodic, 148–150
  musical, 142–151. *see also specific types*
  reduction of chords for, 128
  Roman numeral, with inversion symbols,
    136–138, 137*t*
Andante, 15
angle(s)
  key signatures, 157–158
  in music notation, 157, 157*f*
  in musical calligraphy, 157–158, 157*f*
arpeggiation, 1, 145
ascending intervals, writing of, 115
asymmetrical meters, 27
augment, 39
augmented interval, 107
  doubly, 108
augmented triad, 123
aural applications, 32–46. *see also specific types,*
    e.g., sight singing
  metric transcription, 38–40
  rhythmic reading, 32–38
  sight singing, 93–102

Bach, J.S., 1, 147
  Chorale No. 14 "O Herre Gott, dein göttich
    Wort," 143
  Chorale No. 22 "Schmücke dich, o liebe
    Seele," 143
  Suite for Solo Cello No. 1, Mvt. 3, 147
  Suite in E minor for Lute, BWV 996, V,
    "Bourée," 72
  Suite No. 1 for 'Cello, 24
  Two-Part Invention No. 1, 148

backslash through number, 135
barline, 11, 20
bass, 127, 128
  Alberti, 145
  figured, 133–136, 135*t*
    defined, 133
bass clef, 51, 51*f*
basso continuo, 134–136
beaming, 10–11, 160, 160*f*
  in simple and compound meter, 23–24
beat(s), 9
  divided, in rhythmic reading
    for compound meters, 36*t*
    for simple meters, 33*t*
  in rhythmic reading
    for compound meters, 36*t*
    for simple meters, 33, 33*t*, 34
  subdivided, 33–35
    in rhythmic reading
      for compound meters, 36*t*
      for simple meters, 33*t*
  subdivision of, 33–35
beat count, 32, 33
beat note, 18, 18*t*, 21–22, 24–25
beat note value
  in rhythmic reading for compound meters, 36*t*
  in rhythmic reading for simple meters, 33*t*
Beethoven, 1
  Russian Folk Song, Opus 96, 145
  Sonatina in G major, Mvt. II, 22
  Symphony No. 5, Mvt. I, 26
black keys, 47, 48, 48*f*
blocked chord style, 144–145
brace, 51
Brahms, 1
broken chord style, 145

C clef, 52
cadence, 1481–49
cadenza, 25
calligraphy, musical, 10, 157–162
  angles in, 157, 157*f*
cautionary accidentals, 54, 54*f*
change of mode, 83
Chopin, 1
  Nocturne Opus 9, No. 2, 146
  Prelude Opus 28, No. 20, 149

chorale style, 144
chord(s), 116
    defined, 122
    inversion of, 133
    in minor keys, 126
    reduction of, 127–128
        for analysis, 128
        in open spacing, 127
    seventh. *see* seventh chord(s)
    specification of, Roman numerals in,
        126–127
chord style
    blocked, 144–145
    broken, 145
chromatic alterations, of intervals, 107–108
chromatic counting, in identifying specific
        intervals, 109
chromatic half step, 49, 111
chromatic inflections, 93
chromatic scale, 60, 60*f*
    in identifying specific intervals, 109
circle of fifths, 86, 87*f*
clef(s)
    alto, 52*f*
        key signatures and, 82, 82*f*
    bass, 51, 51*f*
    C, 52
    changing of, in middle of passage, 53, 53*f*
    drawing of, 158, 158*f*
    musical notation using, 50–53, 50*f*, 51*f*
    octave, 53, 53*f*
    tenor, 52*f*
        key signatures, 82, 82*f*
    treble, 51, 51*f*
common practice period, 1
common time, 21
compound groupings, 19–20, 36
    reading tuplets within, 38
compound intervals, 112–113
    identifying of, 115
    writing of, 116
compound meter, 22–23
    beaming in, 23–24
    rhythmic reading in, 36–37
    simple meter and, metric transcription
        between, 39–40
    tuplets in, 24–25
conclusive melody, 149
conducting patterns, 20
consonance, 164–165
    perfect, 163
contour(s), 1
    melodic, 150
count
    beat, 32, 33
    chromatic, in identifying specific intervals,
        109
counterpoint, 147
courtesy accidentals, 54, 54*f*
courtesy key signature, 84
crescendo, 5
C-sharp major scale, 63, 64*f*

cut time, 21
cycles per second, 2

d'Arezzo, Guido, 93
degree names
    major scale, 64–65, 64*t*, 65*f*
    natural minor scale, 70*t*
descending intervals, writing of, 116
D-flat major scale, 63, 64*f*
diatonic half step, 49, 79
diatonic interval, 105
diminished interval, 108
    doubly, 108
diminished triad, 123
diminuendo, 5
dissonance, 164–165
divided beat, in rhythmic reading
    for compound meters, 36*t*
    for simple meters, 33*t*
division(s), in rhythmic reading for simple
        meters, 33, 33*t*, 34
divisive rhythm, 19
do solfege, fixed, 94–95
do-based minor solfege, 97
dominant tone, 64, 64*t*, 65*f*
Dorian mode, 61*f*
dot(s), 13
dotted note value, 34
dotted rhythmic values, 12
double dotted note, 13
double sharps, 73
doubly augmented interval, 108
doubly diminished interval, 108
downbeat, 20
duple(s), 23
duple meter, 20, 20*f*
dynamic(s), 1, 4, 161, 161*f*
dynamic markings, 4

eighth note, 10
embellishing tones, 144
enharmonic relationship, 49
enharmonically equivalent, 49
enharmonically respelled, 49
equal temperament, 49
"Every Good Boy Does Fine," 54

fermata, 25
fifth(s)
    circle of, 86, 87*f*
    perfect, 106*t*
    visual recognition of, 105*t*
figured bass, 133–136, 135*t*
    defined, 133
figured bass symbols, 133–134, 135*t*
first inversion, 133
first inversion seventh chord
    figured bass symbols for, 135*t*
    inversion symbols for, 137*t*
first inversion triad
    figured bass symbols for, 135*t*
    inversion symbols for, 137*t*

five-line staff, 11
fixed do solfege, 94–95
flag(s), 10
    drawing of, 159, 159*f*
flat(s), 48*f*
    angle of, 157
    order of, 79–80, 80*f*
flat key signatures, 79–80, 80*f*
flat major key signatures, 79–80, 80*f*
fourth(s)
    defined, 104
    perfect, 106*t*
    visual recognition of, 105*t*
frequency(ies), 2, 3*f,* 163
fully diminished seventh chords, 125*t,* 126
functional tertian harmony, 122
fundamental, 164

G major scale, 63, 63*f*
general intervals, 103–105
    inversional relationships of, 113
    visual recognition of, 105*t*
generic intervals, 103–105
grand staff, 51, 51*f*

hairpin(s), 5
half diminished seventh chords, 125*t,* 126
half note, 10, 158
half step, 48, 49, 60, 105
    chromatic, 49, 111
    diatonic, 49, 79
    on musical staff, 53–54, 53*f*
Handel, Sonata VII for Flute and Basso
        Continuo, Mvt. II, 136
harmonic(s), 164
harmonic analysis, 142–148
    musical texture and, 142–148
harmonic intervals, 103, 111
harmonic minor scale, 71, 71*f*
harmonic reduction, 144
harmonic rhythm, 143
harmonic structure, 147
harmony
    functional tertian, 122
    implied, 147
    tonal, 122
Hayden, 1
Hertz (Hz), 2
Hertz, Heinrich, 2
homophonic texture, 143–146
Hymn of St. Joannes, 93, 93*f*
Hz (Hertz), 2

implied harmony, 147
inconclusive melody, 149
indexing, tonally, 98
inflection(s), chromatic, 93
interval(s), 103–121
    above given pitch, writing of, 115
    ascending, writing of, 115
    augmented, 107
        doubly, 108

    below given pitch, writing of, 116
    chromatic alterations of, 107–108
    compound, 112–113
        identifying of, 115
        writing of, 116
    descending, writing of, 116
    diatonic, 105
    diminished, 108
        doubly, 108
    general, 103–105
        inversional relationships of, 113
        visual recognition of, 105*t*
    generic, 103–105
    harmonic, 103, 111
    identifying, 109–111
        chromatic counting in, 109
        scales in, 109–110
    inversion of, 113–115
    known, identifying of, in relation to unknown
        intervals, 110–111
    major, 106–107, 106*t*
    melodic, 103, 111
    minor, 106–107, 106*t*
    within overtone series, 164–165
    perfect, 106, 106*t*
    qualities of, inversional relationships of, 114
    simple, 112–113
    specific. *see* specific intervals
    types of, 103
    unknown, identifying of, in relation to known
        intervals, 110–111
    writing, 115–116
interval numbers, 103–105
inversion(s)
    of chords, 133
    first, 133
        inversion symbols for, 137*t*
        seventh chord
            figured bass symbols for, 135*t*
            inversion symbols for, 137*t*
        triad for, figured bass symbols for, 135*t*
    in identifying specific intervals, 114
    of intervals, 113–115
    second, 133
        seventh chord
            figured bass symbols for, 135*t*
            inversion symbols for, 137*t*
        triad for, figured bass symbols for, 135*t*
    third, 133
        seventh chord
            figured bass symbols for, 135*t*
            inversion symbols for, 137*t*
inversion symbols, 137*t*
    Roman numeral analysis with, 136–138, 137*t*
inversional relationships
    of general intervals, 113
    of interval qualities, 114
Ionian mode, 61*f,* 70

key(s)
    black, 47, 47*f*
    major

key signatures for, 78
movable do solfege for, 95, 95*t*
minor
commonly found chords in, 126
less commonly found chords in, 126
sharp, 79, 79*f*
white, 47, 47*f*
key signatures, 78–94
for alto and tenor clefs, 82, 82*f*
in angles, 157–158
courtesy, 84
described, 78
flat major, 79–80, 80*f*
for major keys, 78
memorizing, 84–87
minor, 80–81, 80*f*
notating, 81–82, 81*f*
sharp major, 79, 79*f*
key signature tool, 173
major, 85, 90–91
minor, 86, 90–91
keyboard
modern, specific pitch and, 49–50, 49*f*
musical, 47–59. *see also* musical keyboard

"la"-based minor solfege, 96
Largo, 15
leading tone, 64, 64*t*, 65*f*
ledger lines, 52
letter names, 47
Locrian mode, 61*f*
Lydian mode, 61*f*

major intervals, 106–107, 106*t*
major key(s)
key signatures for, 78
movable do solfege for, 95, 95*t*
major key signature tool, 85
major scales, 62–64, 62*f*–64*f*
C-sharp, 63, 64*f*
degree names, 64–65, 64*t*, 65*f*
D-flat, 63, 64*f*
G, 63, 63*f*
in identifying specific intervals, 190–110
minor scales and, relationships between, 82–84, 83*f*
tendency tones in, 69*f*
major second (M2), 106*t*
major seventh (M7), 106*t*
major sixth (M6), 106*t*
major third (M3), 106*t*
major triad, 123
measure(s), 11, 12, 21
melodic analysis, 148–150
melodic contour in, 150
phrase in, 148–149
melodic contour, 150
melodic intervals, 103, 111
melodic minor scales, 71–72, 71*f*, 72*f*
melody(ies)
conclusive, 149
inconclusive, 149

meter(s), 20
asymmetrical, 27
compound. *see* compound meter
duple, 20, 20*f*
mixed, 27
quadruple, 20, 20*f*
simple. *see* simple meter
triple, 20, 20*f*
types of, 20, 20*f*
metric transcription, 38–40
between simple and compound meters, 39–40
metronome, 14
microtone, 105–106
Middle C, 51*f*, 52, 158
minor intervals, 106–107, 106*t*
minor key(s)
commonly found chords in, 126
less commonly found chords in, 126
minor key signature(s), 80–81, 80*f*
minor key signature tool, 86
minor scale, natural, 62
minor scales, 70–73, 70*f*, 70*t*, 71*f*
harmonic, 71, 71*f*
in identifying specific intervals, 190–110
major scales and, relationships between, 82–84, 83*f*
melodic, 71–72, 71*f*, 72*f*
movable solfege for, 95–97
natural, 62, 70–73, 70*f*, 70*t*, 71*f*
spelling, 72–73, 73*f*
minor second (m2), 106*t*
minor seventh (m7), 106*t*
minor sixth (m6), 106*t*
minor solfege
do-based, 97
"la"-based, 96
minor triad, 123
mixed meter, 27
Mixolydian mode, 61*f*
mode(s)
change of, 83
types of, 61–62, 61*f*, 70, 86
Moderato, 15
modern keyboard, specific pitch and, 49–50, 49*f*
modulation, 148
monophonic texture, 146–147
motive(s), 1
rhythmic, 42, 104
movable do solfege, for major keys, 95, 95*t*
movable solfege, for minor scales, 95–97
Mozart, Wolfgang Amadeus, 1
Clarinet Concerto in A Major K, 622, 20
Piano Sonata in C Major K, 545, 152–156
Sonata K, 545, Mvt. I, 2, 6–8, 145, 146
Symphony No. 40, Mvt. I, 9, 41, 104, 150
multiple stops, 147
music
defined, 1
non-metered, 25–26
tonal, 1

music calligraphy, 157–162
  angles in, 157, 157*f*
music triads, 1
musical analysis, 142–151
  harmonic analysis, 142–148
  melodic analysis, 148–150
musical calligraphy, 10, 157–162
  angles in, 157, 157*f*
musical keyboard, 47–59
  black keys, 47, 48, 48*f*
  white keys, 47, 47*f*
musical notation, 157–162
  angles in, 157, 157*f*
  using staves and clefs, 50–53, 50*f*, 51*f*
musical performance
  proportionate division in, 18–19
  proportionate subdivision in, 18–19
musical staff, whole and half steps on, 53–54, 53*f*
musical texture
  defined, 142
  harmonic analysis and, 142–148
  homophonic, 143–146
  monophonic, 146–147
  polyphonic, 147–148
  types of, 143–148

natural(s), 48*f*
natural minor scale, 62, 70–73, 70*f*, 70*t*, 71*f*
ninth(s), 112
non-chord tone, 146
non-chord tones, 144
non-metered music, 25–26
notation(s)
  musical, 157–162
    angles in, 157, 157*f*
    using staves and clefs, 50–53, 50*f*, 51*f*
  rhythmic, 9–10, 40
note(s), 3, 10. *see also specific notes, e.g.,* sixty-
    fourth note
  beat, 18, 18*t*, 21–22, 24–25
    value of, in rhythmic reading
      for compound meters, 36*t*
      for simple meters, 33*t*
  double dotted, 13
  drawing of, 159, 159*f*
  eighth, 10
  half, 10, 158
  proportional values of, 18
  quarter, 10
  sixteenth, 10
  sixty-fourth, 10
  thirty-second, 10
  whole, 158
note value(s)
  dotted, 34
  rhythmic, 18, 18*t*
  in rhythmic reading for simple meters, 33, 34,
    34*t*
  tied, 34
notehead(s), 10, 40, 50
  filled, drawing of, 158, 158*f*
number(s), opus, 145–146

octave(s), 48, 112
  described, 104
  perfect, 106*t*
  visual recognition of, 105*t*
octave clef, 53, 53*f*
octave equivalence, 48, 112, 113, 127, 164
open spacing, reduction of chords in, 127
opus numbers, 145–146
oral tradition, 9
order of flats, 79–80, 80*f*
order of sharps, 79, 79*f*
ottava, 52*t*
ottava bassa, 52*t*
ottava signs, 52*t*
overtone, 164
overtone series, 122, 163–164, 163*f*
  intervals within, 164–165

parallel relationship, 83
perfect consonance, 163
perfect fifth (P5), 106*t*
perfect fourth (P4), 106*t*
perfect intervals, 106, 106*t*
perfect octave (P8), 106*t*
perfect pitch, 94
perfect unison (PU), 106*t*
phrase, 1
  in melodic analysis, 148–149
Phrygian mode, 61*f*
pitch(es), 2, 3, 47–59
  given
    writing intervals above, 115–116
    writing intervals below, 116
  musical, reading of, 54–55
  perfect, 94
  relative, 94
  specific, 54
    modern keyboard and, 49–50, 49*f*
pitch class, 48
pitch class letter names, 95
pitch names, 47
polymeter, 40
polyphonic texture, 147–148
pop/jazz chord symbols, 125–126, 125*t*
Presto, 15
proportion, in simple meter, 21–22
proportional values, of notes and rests, 18,
    18*t*
proportionate division, in musical
    performance, 18–19
proportionate subdivision, in musical
    performance, 18–19
pulse, 9

quadruple, 23
quadruple meter, 20, 20*f*
quality(ies)
  interval, inversional relationships of,
    114
  of triad, 123
quarter notes, 10
quindicesima, 52*t*

quindicesimbassa, 52*t*
quintuplet, 13

reading, rhythmic, 32–38. *see also* rhythmic
reading
realization, 134–136
recognition, of specific intervals, 109–111
reduction
harmonic, 144
rhythmic, 40–42, 104
relative pitch, 94
relative relationship, 82, 84
rest(s), 11–12
drawing of, 159, 159*f*
proportional values of, 18, 18*t*
rhythm, 3, 9–17
divisive, 19
harmonic, 143
rhythmic motive, 42, 104
rhythmic notation, 9–10, 40
rhythmic note value, 18, 18*t*
rhythmic proportions, 18, 18*t*
rhythmic reading, 32–38
in compound meter, 36–37
in simple meter, 32–36
rhythmic reduction, 40–42, 104
rhythmic values
dotted, 12
tied, 12
Rigoletto, Act II, 29, 30
Roman numeral(s), in chord specification,
126–127
Roman numeral analysis, with inversion
symbols, 136–138, 137*t*
root, 122
root position, 122
root position seventh chord
figured bass symbols for, 135*t*
inversion symbols for, 137*t*
root position triad
figured bass symbols for, 135*t*
inversion symbols for, 137*t*

SATB. *see* soprano, alto, tenor, and bass
(SATB)
scale(s), 1
chromatic, 60, 60*f*
defined, 60
in identifying specific intervals, 109–110
major, 62–64, 62*f*–64*f. see also* major
scales
minor, 70–73, 70*f*, 70*t*, 71*f. see also*
minor scales
scale degree, 63, 103
scale degree numbers, 97–98
Schubert
Moment Musical No. 6, 78
Opus 24, No. 1, 41
Schubert, Franz, 1, 40
second(s), 104
defined, 104
identifying, 109

major, 106*t*
visual recognition of, 105*t*
second inversion, 133
second inversion seventh chord
figured bass symbols for, 135*t*
inversion symbols for, 137*t*
second inversion triad
figured bass symbols for, 135*t*
inversion symbols for, 137*t*
semitone, 60
seventh(s)
major, 106*t*
minor, 106*t*
visual recognition of, 105*t*
seventh chord(s), 124, 124*t*
first inversion
figured bass symbols for, 135*t*
inversion symbols for, 137*t*
fully diminished, 125*t*, 126
half diminished, 125*t*, 126
inversion of, 133
root position
figured bass symbols for, 135*t*
inversion symbols for, 137*t*
second inversion
figured bass symbols for, 135*t*
inversion symbols for, 137*t*
third inversion
figured bass symbols for, 135*t*
inversion symbols for, 137*t*
sharp(s), 48*f*
angle of, 157
double, 73
order of, 79, 79*f*
sharp keys, 79, 79*f*
sharp major key signatures, 79, 79*f*
sight singing, 93–102
application, 98
fixed do solfege, 94–95
pitch class letter names in, 95
scale degree numbers in, 97–98
signature(s)
key, 78–94. *see also* key signatures
time, 20, 22, 23
simple groupings, 19–20
reading tuplets within, 37–38
simple intervals, 112–113
simple meter, 21, 21*t*, 25
beaming in, 23–24
compound meter and, metric transcription
between, 39–40
proportion in, 21–22
rhythmic reading in, 32–36
sixteenth note, 10
sixth(s), 104
major, 106*t*
minor, 106*t*
visual recognition of, 105*t*
sixty-fourth note, 10
slur(s), 161
solfege, 93
fixed do, 94–95

minor
    do-based, 97
    "la"-based, 96
    movable
        do-based, for major keys, 95, 95t
        for minor scales, 95–97
soprano, alto, tenor, and bass (SATB), 143
sound, basics of, 2–5, 3f
spacing, open, reduction of chords in, 127
specific intervals, 105–107, 106t
    chromatic counting of, 109
    identifying of, inversions in, 114
    writing and recognizing, 109–111
specific pitch, 54
    modern keyboard and, 49–50, 49f
spelling minor scales, 72–73, 73f
staff(ves), 158
    five-line, 11
    grand, 51, 51f
    musical notation using, 50–53, 50f, 51f
    treble clef, 54
    whole and half steps on, 53–54, 53f
staff system, 51
stem(s), 10, 158
step(s)
    half. see half step
    whole, 48, 49
        on musical staff, 53–54, 53f
stop(s), multiple, 147
subdivided beat, 33–35
    in rhythmic reading
        for compound meters, 36t
        for simple meters, 33t
subdominant tone, 64, 64t, 65f
submediant tone, 64, 64t, 65f
supertonic tone, 64, 64t, 65f

tempo, 14–15, 22
tendency tones, 69–70, 69f
    in major scales, 69f
tenor clefs, 52f
    key signatures and, 82, 82f
tenth(s), 112
texture(s)
    defined, 142
    homophonic, 143–146
    monophonic, 146–147
    musical. see musical texture
    polyphonic, 147–148
    voice, 160, 160f
third(s)
    defined, 104
    major, 106t
    visual recognition of, 105t
third inversion, 133
third inversion seventh chord
    figured bass symbols for, 135t
    inversion symbols for, 137t
thirty-second note, 10
tie(s), 161
tied note value, 34
tied rhythmic values, 12

timbre, 3
time
    common, 21
    cut, 21
time signature, 20, 22, 23, 159
tonal harmony, 122
tonal music, 1
tonally indexing, 98
tone(s)
    dominant, 64, 64t, 65f
    embellishing, 144
    leading, 64, 64t, 65f
    non-chord, 144, 146
    subdominant, 64, 64t, 65f
    submediant, 64, 64t, 65f
    supertonic, 64, 64t, 65f
    tendency, 69–70, 69f
        in major scale, 69f
tonic, 64, 64t, 65f
tonicization pattern, 98
transcription, metric, 38–40
transposing instrument, 82
transposition, 63
treble clef, 51, 51f
treble clef staff, 54
triad(s), 1, 122–123
    augmented, 123
    defined, 122
    diminished, 123
    first inversion
        figured bass symbols for, 135t
        inversion symbols for, 137t
    major, 123
    minor, 123
    quality of, 123
    root position
        figured bass symbols for, 135t
        inversion symbols for, 137t
    second inversion
        figured bass symbols for, 135t
        inversion symbols for, 137t
triple, 23
triple meter, 20, 20f
triplet(s), 13
tritone, 107, 165
tuplet(s), 13–14
    in compound meter, 24–25
    reading of
        within compound groupings, 38
        within simple groupings, 37–38

unison(s), 104
    defined, 103
    perfect, 106t
    visual recognition of, 105t
upbeat, 20, 22
Ut queant laxis, 93, 93f

Varése, Edgard, 1
Verdi, Giuseppe, 1, 39
Vivaldi, 1
    "Spring" from The Four Seasons, Mvt. I, 9

voice(s), in musical texture, 142
voice textures, 160, 160*f*

white keys, 47, 47*f*
whole notes, 158
whole step, 48, 49
    on musical staff, 53–54, 53*f*

writing, of intervals
    above given pitch, 115–116
    below given pitch, 116
    specific, 109–111